Quiet Moments

for Homeschool

Moms *and* Dads

Quiet Moments
for Homeschool
Moms *and* Dads

Vicki A. Brady

VINE
BOOKS

SERVANT PUBLICATIONS
ANN ARBOR, MICHIGAN

Vine Books is an imprint of Servant Publications especially designed to serve evangelical Christians.

Unless otherwise noted, all Scripture verses were taken from the New American Standard Bible, © The Lockman Foundation, 1960, 1962, 1963, 1968, 1971, 1972, 1973, 1975, 1977.

Except for stories involving the author's immediate family, the people and situations in this book are compilations of characters and events.

Published by Servant Publications
P.O. Box 8617
Ann Arbor, Michigan 48107

Cover design: Paz Design Group, Salem, Oregon
Cover photograph: © Jill Sabella, FPG International. Used by permission.

99 00 01 02 10 9 8 7 6 5 4 3 2 1

Printed in the United States of America
ISBN 1-56955-166-9

LIBRARY OF CONGRESS CATALOGING-IN-PUBLICATION DATA

Brady, Vicki A.
    Quiet moments for homeschool moms and dads / Vicki A. Brady.
        p.   cm.
    Includes index.
    ISBN 1-56955-166-9 (alk. paper)
    1. Parents Prayer-books and devotions—English.   2. Home schooling
Prayer-books and devotions—English.   I. Title.
BV4529.B69   1999   99-32819
242'.645—dc21   CIP

This book is dedicated to
moms, dads, aunts, uncles,
singles, and grandparents around the world
who have
sacrificed greatly to
homeschool their loved ones.

A Note From the Author

Don't skip this page! The people I would like to thank are people you need to get to know. Their inspiration, love, dedication, and support have helped to make this book possible. A "humongous" thank-you goes to:

The Lord Jesus Christ! Without you this book wouldn't be possible. Thank you for the trials in my life. Through every learning experience you were there, comforting, teaching, encouraging, and inspiring me.

My husband Terry: I love you! You took on the responsibilities of ten people in order to help me finish this book. I will miss seeing you in my apron.

My children, Emily, Sam, Ben, James, Helen, Connie, and Anna: For letting me use your stories and for being so forgiving and easy on Dad while I was writing.

Marc, Susan, Anneli, and Amy Horner: Thank you, Marc, for living without your women for a few days while they stayed with me. Thank you, Susan, Anneli, and Amy, for watching my children, playing games, fixing meals, and washing my kitchen floor so I could write and not feel guilty.

Mary Mangum: A new friend who kept my children in Valentines, soap, and lots of other goodies while they were without a mom.

To all the homeschooling families in my life: Thank you for letting me use your stories (your names have been changed, of course!).

ONE

Every Family Is a Homeschool Family

And you shall teach them diligently to your sons and shall talk of them when you sit in your house and when you walk by the way and when you lie down and when you rise up.

DEUTERONOMY 6:7

Have you ever stopped to consider the fact that, one way or another, every family is a "homeschooling family"? The home is where our children learn to walk, talk, feed themselves, and use the potty-chair. At home they learn how to make their beds, share their toys, and feed the dog. By age four most children can recite their ABCs, count to ten, name simple shapes, and recognize at least five colors. Who taught them all of these things? You did!

The most important lessons that a child ever learns will probably be taught at home. Even so, each parent must determine before God how much of their child's education is to be delegated to a public school, entrusted to private schools or tutors, or kept "in house." Depending on your circumstances, God may give you freedom to use any of these means to educate your children. Still, responsibility for the education of children rests squarely on the shoulders of their parents. And since most important lessons are taught at home, all families have one thing in common—they homeschool!

There is another responsibility that all parents share. As the preceding verse indicates, each of us has been given the privilege—been commanded by God, in fact—to take responsibility for the religious education of our children. For years I assumed that the religious education of my children was the church's responsibility. Deuteronomy tells us differently.

We cannot expect our children to spiritually grow or excel on an hour or two a week at church. If it takes twenty hours a week to provide a proper academic foundation, how many hours will it take for a solid spiritual one? Knowing God, learning his ways, and getting his wisdom is something that we as parents cannot afford to delegate. This is one area in which every parent *must* be a homeschooling parent!

Today's Prayer

Dear Father, thank you for the time you are giving us to influence and instruct our children, both academically and spiritually. Remind us of the importance and priority of each.

Just for Today

Make a list of the academic areas on which you want to focus: math, reading, science, language, art, history, or writing. Then make a list of the spiritual areas in which you want your children to progress: character development, Bible memorization, applying Scripture to everyday life, or studying the heroes of the faith. Make lesson plans for both.

TWO

The Teacup

Do not lay up for yourselves treasures upon earth, where moth and rust destroy, and where thieves break in and steal. But lay up for yourselves treasures in heaven, where neither moth nor rust destroys, and where thieves do not break in or steal; for where your treasure is, there will your heart be also.

MATTHEW 6:19-21

I love sipping coffee or tea from fine china. Somehow the delicate porcelain rim always makes the drink taste better. While living in New Zealand we got a deal on a tea set, and even managed to ship it back to the States without a chip. Between seven children and seven subsequent moves, however, each of my four china cups and saucers was broken beyond repair.

One year I was given a beautiful china cup and saucer with fourteen-carat gold trim. My children tried very hard to take care of the beautiful dishes—until my three-year-old's elbow connected with a water glass that sent my cup and saucer sailing off the table.

Dead silence. Tears brimmed in my daughter's eyes and everyone waited to see what I would do. It was at that moment that I remembered my mother-in-law, Mary, whose set of antique goblets, which had been in the family forever, were used at a Christmas dinner. While I was drying dishes after the meal, one goblet slipped out of my hand and shattered on her kitchen floor.

As a new bride anxious to fit into the family, I was horrified at what had just happened. Just then Mary did an amazing thing. She picked up a matching goblet, held it high above her head, and said, "Vicki, you are far more valuable to me and the Lord than a glass could ever be. If it will make you feel any better I'll break this one as well and we can clean it up together." I've loved her ever since.

After telling that story to my children and giving my daughter a squeeze, I cleaned up yet another cup and saucer. Given the choice, I would much rather drink coffee from plastic mugs with my children gathered around me than from the most expensive china, alone.

Today's Prayer

Dear Father, someday my children will be grown and I may have a china cupboard filled with delicate cups and saucers, but for now, thank you for the most important treasure I have in my home—my children. What a joy it is to teach them, grow with them, laugh with them, and even cry together over broken china.

Just for Today

Have a tea party with your children. Even boys will enjoy it!

THREE
A New Direction

The mind of man plans his way but the Lord directs his steps.

PROVERBS 16:9

"Your mother has terminal cancer." The words hit my husband like a blast of Arctic air. Only weeks earlier Mary had been well, doing grandmotherly things and planning a spring visit to our home. Now she lay in a Tucson hospital with less than six months to live.

When she was stable enough to travel, we had her flown to our mountain home in Colorado. As the ambulance opened its door, we gasped at the weakened body of the woman who only six months earlier had spent Christmas with us, full of vim, vigor, and a "shop till you drop" approach to life.

Terry's mother, Mary, and father, Bob, came to live with us at the height of our school year. Although I dearly loved them and wanted them with us, the care they required kept me from spending the time I needed to in school ... or so I thought.

At first I began to panic. Mentally I calculated the number of days needed to complete each subject, constantly reevaluating how many lessons and days I could squeeze together. Even during the times when I was able to sit with my children and begin class, I was frequently interrupted by questions like,

"How come Grandma can't sit up anymore?"

"What is death?"

"What is heaven like?"

Answers to these questions and many more like them began to eat up even more of my valuable teaching time.

One morning during my quiet time with the Lord I voiced

my frustration. "Lord, why have you allowed this interruption to my school?"

Gently and peaceably, the Lord said to me, "Interruption? What interruption? I see only direction!"

From that day on we began to learn about cancer, death, dying, heaven, and eternal life.

About two weeks later during family devotions, four-year-old Helen raised her hand. "I've been thinking," she began. "I know that Grandma is a Christian and when she dies she's gonna be with Jesus. If I ever die I wanna be with both of them, but I don't know how!" Minutes later we had the privilege of leading our daughter to a saving knowledge of Jesus Christ.

Today's Prayer

O Father, on days when I am tempted to complain about the "interruptions" life brings to our school schedule, help me remember Grandma and little Helen. Some "interruptions" reap eternal rewards.

Just for Today

As you begin your day with your well-laid plans, watch to see what new direction the Lord gives you by way of unexpected phone calls, visits, and even illnesses.

FOUR
Stressed by Success

There is an appointed time for everything. And there is a time for every event under heaven.

ECCLESIASTES 3:1

"I'm thinking of enrolling my children in a charter school after the holidays."

What a shock! Christine had successfully homeschooled all six of her children, including one who had gone on to get her degree in engineering and a seven-year-old who was reading at a fifth-grade level. She was an inspiration, not only to me but to literally hundreds of other families. Why would she want to quit?

She didn't, Christine explained. It was just that she didn't have time to teach anymore! Church leaders, noticing her homeschooling success, had prevailed upon her to share her wisdom, creativity, and methods with their Sunday school department. One thing led to another, and soon she was speaking to and teaching groups of people on a regular basis. She needed to quit homeschooling because she was so good at homeschooling!

Over the next four cups of coffee Christine told me that she felt pulled in many directions. Her church and various home-school groups were asking for her help, and she knew it was important to support homeschooling parents. Yet tension was mounting between her and her husband, and she felt guilty about how little time she was spending with her youngest three. The only solution seemed to be to send her children to a good charter school, but was that what the Lord wanted?

I just listened as Christine sorted things out. She knew that her primary responsibility was to her family. It was apparent that her heart longed for the good old days, when she had had time to teach her children and care for her family. In the end, Christine concluded that it was a matter of timing. She indeed was destined to help others with their teaching and ministries— just not now.

It was a hard decision. Christine was turning down an opportunity for prestige, money, and the satisfaction that comes from making a difference in a bigger world. There will be time for that later, once her children are grown. For now, she's back doing what she loves—and what she knows God wants her to do.

Today's Prayer

Dear Lord, thank you for giving us the gifts we need to home-school our children—and to make a difference in the world around us. Don't let us jump ahead of your will or your timing for our lives.

Just for Today

Is there any ministry or activity in your life that interferes with your most important job: being a godly parent? Ask God what he would have you do to correct the situation.

FIVE

The Bee Sting

He ... is the blessed and only Sovereign, the King of Kings and Lord of Lords.

1 TIMOTHY 6:15b

O ne of the most misunderstood doctrines of the church today is the sovereignty of God. According to *Webster's Dictionary*, the word *sovereign* means "above or superior to all others; supreme in power or rank; of or being a ruler; independent of all others; excellent."

First Timothy tells us that God is the only sovereign (see 1 Tim 6:15-16). This means that he rules everything: earthly kings, events, and even nature. This lesson was brought home during a recent bee invasion.

We were sitting on our deck when all at once five or six bees began buzzing around us. The children started to panic, swat, and duck, until my husband, Terry, asked them to stop and listen. Just days before we had talked about the sovereignty of God in devotions, and now was the time to practically apply that lesson. Terry reminded us all that if God is sovereign over nature, then even a bee can't sting us unless he allows it.

"But what if he allows it?" one child asked in horror.

Before my husband could answer, one of the other children said, "Well, then we would have to apply Romans 8:28, 'For we know that all things work together for good to them that love God, to them that are called according to his purpose.'"

About that time one of the children began to pray out loud. "Dear Lord, I know you are sovereign over these bees, and I know they won't sting me if you tell them not to. Would you please talk to them and tell them to just go away?"

Within minutes the bees were gone and we all sat in awe. Moments later a tiny voice piped up, "Now I wonder if this also applies to spiders!"

Today's Prayer

Dear Heavenly Father, thank you for commanding even the bees in the air. Help our children to never forget that whatever happens in their lives, you are in control and you will work your plan through it.

Just for Today

Talk about bees in school today and serve your children a snack of butter and honey on bread.

SIX

The Painted Face

*And let not your adornment be merely external—braiding the
hair, and wearing gold jewelry, or putting on dresses; but let it be
the hidden person of the heart, with the imperishable quality of a
gentle and quiet spirit, which is precious in the sight of God.*

1 PETER 3:3-4

"Thirty minutes before we leave for church!" I announced before heading to the bathroom to "put on
my face." A pre-Christmas gift certificate had allowed me to
get some brand-new products including lipstick, eye shadow,
and blush.

As I took my makeup case out of the cupboard I immediately knew something was wrong. Upon closer examination I
was shocked to discover that my new shadow applicator was totally covered with brown gunk. The blush brush was so full of
powder that it let off a puff of smoke in my face as I tried to
apply it to my cheeks. And my lipstick! The joy of using a new
lipstick is in the defined point at the top. This tube had a tip as
round as a marble.

My children had committed the unpardonable sin. They had
played with mom's makeup! Just as I was about to commit another unpardonable sin, the Lord reminded me of the "fast."

Our whole family had agreed to go on a video and computer
"fast" the previous week. For some time my husband and I had
been concerned about the amount of time the children were
wasting on these two forms of entertainment. Chores were
neglected or only half-done, no one was reading for pleasure,
and the children were not playing with one another as much as

19

they should. We all agreed to go on a voluntary one-week fast and not touch any electronic form of entertainment.

The results were refreshing, and exceeded our expectations. The children drew pictures; played board games; went to the library; read books; wrote poetry; sent letters; and even wrote, directed, and starred in a family play! The story line was simple, but the costuming very creative. As I now recalled, they had mentioned that they needed makeup....

My anger abated as I remembered the play, their creativity and joy, and the harmony we had all enjoyed over the past seven days. My makeup was a small price to pay for such a wonderful week.

Today's Prayer

O Father, I never said a word about my makeup to the children. Remind me every morning when I use it (in spite of the deep gouges, marbled tips, and gooped-up applicators) to thank you for my children's creativity.

Just for Today

If you have makeup, let your children use some of the old stuff to transform themselves into clowns, lions, or puppy dogs.

SEVEN

Fence In, Fence Out

*So we built the wall and the whole wall was joined together to half
its height, for the people had a mind to work.*

NEHEMIAH 4:6

Living on a ranch in Colorado, we learned firsthand about
the fencing laws each state adopts. Some are "fence in"
states, which means that if you own livestock in that state, by
law you are responsible for maintaining good fences to keep
your animals on your land. If a critter escapes and causes damage to your neighbor's property, you are financially liable.

If you live in a "fence out" state, it is up to you as a land-
owner to put fences up if you do not want animals wandering
onto your property. In these states, if your neighbor's cattle
meander into your garden and eat all your veggies, your only
recourse is to replant your lettuce.

Christian parents need to adopt a kind of "fence out"
policy when it comes to their children. Our children need spiritual fences—biblical standards that parents establish in the
home, which in turn shape the worldview of our families.
Without these standards, our children will soon find themselves
in situations that bring heartache and destruction. It's also important to keep these "fences" in good repair through frequent,
positive reinforcement. This helps to guard against any tempta-
tion our children may face in breaking down fences that keep
them away from drugs, immorality, and bad companions. We
need to teach our children that spiritual fences are not to be
feared and resisted. They are there for our guidance and protection. To avoid them or try to tear them down can harm us.

Children need to build their own fences, too, to keep out harmful critters that would turn them from their walk with the Lord. Memorizing God's Word is the very foundation of a spiritual fence that can hold back humanism and heresy.

As parents we need to remember that, no matter how solidly we build our spiritual fences, there will be some children who won't rest until they find a breach. Still, that does not release us from our responsibility to establish and protect needed spiritual walls.

Today's Prayer

Father God, reinforce our fences and help us find the breaches in our walls.

Just for Today

If you have a fence around your property, take a walk around it with your children and look for places needing repair. Talk to them about the fence, and ask them what it's supposed to keep out and what it's supposed to keep in. At the same time, help them to identify areas in their spiritual fences that need attention.

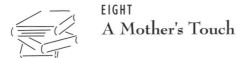

EIGHT

A Mother's Touch

Jotham was twenty-five years old when he became king, and he reigned sixteen years in Jerusalem. And his mother's name was Jerushah the daughter of Zadok. And he did right in the sight of the Lord.

2 CHRONICLES 27:1-2a

The first time I read this passage as a teenager, I was so impressed with Jotham's mother that I thought about naming my firstborn daughter Jerushah. What a woman she must have been! Her influence in her son's life earned her eternal recognition in the Scriptures, which acknowledge that "Jotham became mighty because he ordered his ways before the Lord his God" (v. 6).

If we look closely at the Book of 2 Chronicles, which records biographical information about the kings of Israel and Judah, there appears to be a connection between the number of kings who "did right in the eyes of the Lord" and the influence their mothers had in their lives. Of the nine kings who did what was "right in the eyes of the Lord," six mention the king's mother. Of the eight kings who were wicked, only one mother's name is given.

Further study shows that age alone didn't seem to make a difference between who served God and who didn't. Joash was seven and Josiah was eight when they became godly kings. Jehoiachin, on the other hand, was a wicked king at the age of eight, and Manasseh began his evil reign at age twelve. Two-thirds of the kings began to rule when they were in their twenties—half served God, and half didn't.

Raising children is not an exact science. There are no guarantees that our children will choose to serve the Lord, but there are some things we can do to influence them in that direction. Homeschooling is one of those things. On days when you begin to wonder if you are spinning your wheels with your children, keep in mind people like Jerushah and Jotham. Scripture records *both* their names, which tells me God thought they were both very important. Similarly, he has chosen you to be the mother of your children. It is your touch that they need in their lives, and homeschooling is giving you more time to influence your children for the kingdom of God.

Today's Prayer

O Father, help us not to underestimate the power in a mother's touch. Show us how to make the best of the little time we have with our children.

Just for Today

Hug your children, stroke their hair, and whisper in their ears just how much you love them.

NINE

The Real Enemy

Be of sober spirit, be on the alert. Your adversary, the devil, prowls about like a roaring lion, seeking someone to devour.

1 PETER 5:8

The demands of ministry and military life had made ours a truly "mobile home"; in twenty-two years we had moved twenty-six times! Then in 1995 we settled into a wonderful home deep in the Rocky Mountains of Colorado. This was the first house that was truly our own, and I was ready to nest.

Shortly after we had settled in, we began to take regular walks through a nearby cemetery. On one occasion we read the tombstone of an eighteen-year-old man who had died only a couple of years before we moved to the community. Curiosity got the best of us, so while we were in town one day we asked about the circumstances of his death.

We were not prepared for what we discovered. The high school student had been attacked by a mountain lion as he ran around the school track, less than a quarter of a mile from our house. This wonderful mountain on which we had just bought our home was believed to have the highest mountain lion population in the state!

My excitement over our new home faded quickly as one of the locals warned us that a mountain lion could snatch a two-year-old child and carry her a couple of miles before anyone knew she was missing. We were in shock. How could the Lord have put us here? How would we ever be able to protect our children in such a hostile environment?

We started reading all the books we could find about mountain lions, their nature, habits, and snares. Soon we began to relax and let down our guard. It was as though we thought knowing everything about mountain lions made them less of a threat to us. When word came that another "cat" had been seen prowling the streets, our guard went back up.

Scripture describes the devil as a prowling, "roaring lion." Our children must be trained to understand that as long as we are on this earth, we must keep our watch. We need to learn to recognize his ways, his methods, and his snares. Reading about our adversary is not enough—we must stay alert!

Today's Prayer

Dear Father, thank you for the warnings you give about our greatest enemy, Satan. Show us how to prepare our children to be on guard against him.

Just for Today

Have your children draw or cut out pictures of lions and compare his snares and ways to those of our greatest enemy.

TEN

Innocence Lost

Beloved, do not imitate what is evil, but what is good. The one who does good is of God; the one who does evil has not seen God.

3 JOHN 1:11

There is nothing like an outing in the park on a bright, warm spring day. I had declared a holiday one morning and headed over to the swings and teeter-totters with my children. They were having a great time when all of a sudden one of my children, who had just learned how to read, yelled, "Hey, mom, I can read! Listen to this."

He was standing at the top of the slide, where a child had etched some words into the metal. All of a sudden it dawned on me just what those words could be, so I yelled out, "Don't read...."

It was too late. My son, reading loud enough for everyone on the playground to hear, shouted, "It says #%&* @#$!*!!!"

What was I to do? I called him over and explained that those were very bad words and that he must never repeat them. He asked me what they meant. How does one explain such things to a five-year-old?

Strange as it sounds, I was grateful that I was there when my children were first exposed to vulgarity. It gave me the opportunity to teach them how wrong the words were and then to pray with them. We prayed that God might erase those words from their memories, and that the Lord would save whoever was responsible for writing the words. I then thanked God that as a homeschooling mom I was able to deal with these issues at the time they happened rather than after the fact. After crawling up the slide and doing what I could to scratch out the foul language, we went home, a little older and a little wiser.

No matter how carefully we watch over our children, we can't protect them every moment from situations that could rob them of their innocence. We can, however, be available for preventative maintenance and damage control. The minds of our children are too precious for us to leave this task to others.

Today's Prayer

Dear Lord, thank you for being the tireless Guardian and Protector of our children. Help us to protect them when we can—and trust you for the times we can't.

Just for Today

Visit the park and swing, hit a few baseballs, and play with your children. Just be careful about what they read.

ELEVEN

Academics Versus Spirituality

Set your mind on the things above, not on the things that are on earth.

COLOSSIANS 3:2

Recently I was heartbroken to hear about a homeschooled Christian boy who, upon graduation from college at the top of his class, announced to his parents that he no longer believed in God. He went to work for a prestigious company, made a great deal of money, and became addicted to drugs.

The next thing we knew, this young man was diagnosed with AIDS. He returned to his parents' home to die a slow and agonizing death.

The parents, who were pioneers in the homeschool movement, were consumed with regret. They had placed a great deal of emphasis on the academic success of their children. They had believed that it was important to prove to the world that teaching children at home would not produce an academically inferior child. Although they were Christians, they had feared that spending too much time on "religious" things would interfere with their son's academic progress.

Worldly thinking has convinced us that we can have spiritual children or we can have intelligent children but we cannot have both. This idea can cause us to vacillate between spending time on the academic curricula, and concentrating on Bible study and its practical applications to life and character. I submit to you that we *can* and *should* have both.

If we place too high a priority on standardized tests and college entrance exams, our children may excel intellectually yet lack the spiritual reinforcement they need to develop sound character and a servant heart.

On the other hand, if we teach our children to give priority to their walk with the Lord, won't they try to please God in their studies so that they will be ready for the future he has in mind for them? As parents, we need to help our children find the correct balance between feeding the mind and feeding the soul.

Today's Prayer

My Heavenly Father, you alone have given our children the mental abilities to learn, to reason, and to understand. Give them also a thirst for righteousness, for purity, and for godliness. Help us nurture both the spiritual and the academic, each in its proper place.

Just for Today

Take a few minutes to pray with each of your children and encourage them to yield their minds, their hearts, and their spirits to the Lord.

TWELVE

Dream Stealers

*Let no one look down on your youthfulness, but rather in speech,
conduct, love, faith and purity, show yourself an example of those
who believe.*

1 TIMOTHY 4:12

Driving home from a shopping trip in Denver, we heard on
the radio that on the eve of the impeachment vote,
President Clinton had given the order to resume bombing in
Iraq. Just having studied politics and impeachment, one of my
boys literally gasped at the report.

"Mom, he can't do that. The president is trying to get out
of being impeached, and now people are going to die!"

We discussed the subject all the way home. I thought the
topic had been exhausted until one of my sons asked if he
could call the president. I almost blurted out, "Of course not!"
but was stopped when I remembered something I had heard
earlier in the week.

I had interviewed an author named Mike Yaconelli, who
pointed out that we as parents can be "dream stealers." We can
steal the dreams of our children by telling them what they cannot accomplish. We steal their dreams when we tell them they
are not smart enough to try calculus or not agile enough to
take gymnastics or not articulate enough to answer the phone.
While some functions require a degree of proficiency, others
will be accomplished only as we let our children first dream,
then try, and, finally, discover.

My thoughts were interrupted by my son's persistence.
"Mom, I really want to talk to the president and ask him to

stop bombing those people right now."

"Go for it!"

For the next hour my son called number after number, getting mostly answering machines. At times he would reach a human being and would be given another number to try. Finally he reached what sounded like the White House. While he wasn't allowed to speak to the president, he was offered a picture of the White House dog and cat.

When he hung up I expected disappointment to be written all over his face, but it wasn't. He was beaming. "Well, I didn't get to talk to the president, but I did get to the White House. That's a start." With those words he headed up to bed, a contented and satisfied boy.

I never would have guessed that he had the tenacity and boldness to try to accomplish what I believed to be the impossible. His success was in the fact that he tried, did his very best, and came as close to his dream as he could.

Today's Prayer

O Father, teach us to watch for opportunities to become "dream givers" instead of "dream stealers." Help us temper our cautions with encouragement.

Just for Today

Take a few minutes to share with your children all the dreams you had as a child—things like flying, being on stage, or marrying a prince! Then let them share their dreams with you.

THIRTEEN

The Final Exam

Each man's work will become evident; for the day will show it, because it is to be revealed with fire; and the fire itself will test the quality of each man's work.

1 CORINTHIANS 3:13

One day during a math exercise we were supposed to get a ruler and measure things around the house. We found a six-inch ruler and measured things like a peanut, a pencil, and a ring. But this ruler didn't work very well when we tried to measure a book or the rabbit—it was too short. For those things we needed a one-foot ruler. To measure the dog we had to turn to a yardstick, and to get the dimensions of the room we brought out the twenty-five-foot tape measure.

Learning how to measure objects was fun and led me to discuss other ways to measure things and the tools we need to do that. We need measuring cups for cooking, scales for weighing things, and even barometers for atmospheric pressure. Yet how do we measure success, specifically homeschooling success?

Tests can measure success. A standardized achievement test will measure a child's academic progress, but our success as homeschooling parents can be measured only at the final exam, which will take place in heaven.

There will be two parts to this final exam. The first part of the exam will involve just one question: Is Jesus Christ *your* personal Savior? If the answer is "no," the test will be over and we will be dismissed, for eternity. If the answer to that question is "yes," then we will get to move on to the second part of the exam.

During the second half of the exam, all of our deeds will be examined and tested by fire. Labors of love, sacrificial giving, integrity, and steadfastness will shine brighter in the fire. Conversely, some of our other works will only fuel the flames.

Ultimately, our success will be measured by our obedience. On those days when we see no eternal good in what we are doing, when one more person criticizes us for sheltering our children, and when even our children question our sanity, we must obey God and keep doing what we're doing. One day the "final exam" will come for all of us, but this is one exam that we can easily pass if we remain faithful and obedient to the Lord.

Today's Prayer

Most Loving Father, how we look forward to the day when you will put your arm around us, give a gentle squeeze, and say, "Good job, well done, A+!"

Just for Today

Set the table for dinner with only measuring items for utensils. Just try sipping soup through an eyedropper!

FOURTEEN

Suffer the Children

But Jesus said, Suffer little children, and forbid them not, to come unto me: for of such is the kingdom of heaven.

MATTHEW 19:14, KJV

It was one of those days. I wanted to make a dress for one of my girls, and had carefully planned out how many sewing minutes I could squeeze in between math, science, and lunch break. However, I hadn't counted on the dog chewing up a good boot, Anna pulling Connie's hair, and finding my assignment book in a puddle of iced tea.

I lost my cool! I blew up and sent everyone to their bedrooms. How dare they interfere with my well-laid plans! With peace and quiet in the house I sat down and began sewing seams. The house was quiet ... too quiet. Before long I started to feel uncomfortable, though at first I wasn't sure why. I began to pray, and immediately this verse came to mind.

"Suffer the little children to come to me for of such is the kingdom of heaven." The word "suffer" echoed in the canyon of my heart. Why did the Lord use the word "suffer"?

Some aspects of homeschooling and being with our children twenty-four hours a day could be described as suffering. Our own plans, desires, and goals are interrupted or set aside altogether. Money that could be going for a trip to the beach must be diverted to the next curriculum fair. Well-meaning grandparents, family, and friends constantly beg us to reconsider our homeschooling decision before permanent damage is done. We sometimes get discouraged, make mistakes, and feel isolated. All these things can be real sources of suffering.

Putting my sewing down, I called all the children into the living room and apologized for my outburst. Fourteen forgiving arms tried to wrap themselves around me at the same time, and we all fell off the couch and onto the floor, a mass of giggles!

The dress eventually got finished—but not before its intended wearer grew beyond the seams and it became a brand-new hand-me-down!

Today's Prayer

Dear Lord, help me lay my desires and wants at your feet.

Just for Today

If you begin to feel stressed about how much you are not getting done, take even more time to remember the hundreds of projects the Lord has already helped you to accomplish.

FIFTEEN

A Couch Potato

And we know that God causes all things to work together for good to those who love God, to those who are called according to His purpose.

ROMANS 8:28

"Complete bed rest! Think of your floor as being a sea of molten lava. Walk on it only when you have to go to the bathroom."

My midwife was firm. She reminded me of all the horrible things that could happen if my blood pressure wasn't controlled. Years ago I had known a mother with high blood pressure who had died delivering her fourth child. I was scared. This was my fourth child, and I had eight weeks to go before my baby would be born. My blood pressure was high and still rising.

But what about school? I couldn't take two or three months off, but how could I teach my children from a couch? Just thinking about the situation elevated my blood pressure even more!

I was ushered into the living room, where a "nest" was prepared for me on a couch. After I got settled, my daughter came to me carrying her load of books and we began. It wasn't long before I realized that I was able to get more schooling done in a week on the couch than I had been able to do in a month on my feet. I didn't have to interrupt a lesson to put one more load in the washer or make a quick trip to the store for milk. I couldn't clean the house, cook the meals, or even chase the toddlers.

But I *could* read stories to my children, trace their hands on pieces of paper, drill them on their math facts, check their spelling, and help them with their Bible verses. For two months my children had my complete and undivided attention. They knew where to find me at all times!

Eventually the baby came, with only a few complications, and it wasn't long before I was back on my feet. Although I could not return to those days on the couch, the experience helped me to slow down and reevaluate my priorities.

Our children learn what our real priorities are by what we do far more than by what we say. We will "bump" other things out of our schedule to make room for the really important things. By devoting so much of our time to homeschooling, we send a powerful message to our children about what a high priority they are in our lives.

Today's Prayer

Dear Father, help me remove the distractions from my life that interfere with my priorities.

Just for Today

Make a list of the priorities in your life and rate them on a scale of one to ten. Pray about it and then post the list where you can see it daily.

SIXTEEN

Eyes on the Goal

I press on toward the goal for the prize of the upward call of God in Christ Jesus.

PHILIPPIANS 3:14

A s I happily sorted through the holiday mail, quickly opening the Christmas cards, I ran across a newsletter from a homeschooling family who had moved to the West Coast. My delight in hearing from them slowly deteriorated as I carefully read about their current status.

The newsletter listed the age and grade level of each child. According to their parents, the five-year-old was doing second-grade work. The nine-year-old was succeeding with high-school level material, and their twelve-year-old was taking computer classes at the local junior college.

I let my head drop to the table with a thud. Judging from what these parents had been able to accomplish with their kids, I was a "homeschool slug." What had possessed me to think I could ever teach my children? *I should stop what I'm doing, run down to the nearest school, and beg them to take my kids. Better yet, I could let this family adopt my children!*

Just then my husband walked by, took one look at me, and said, "What in the world is wrong with you?" I just shoved the newsletter into his hand and continued to berate myself for my own perceived shortcomings. After reading the newsletter, he chuckled.

At first I was mad. How could he laugh at a time like this?

"You've got your eyes off the goal and on the other runners again!" he grinned. It was true. In every race someone is going to be in front, most will be in the middle, and, of course, one person will be last. Yet God tells us to keep our eyes fixed clearly on the goal, not on the other runners. He is interested in our running and completing the race, not winning it.

Every family homeschools at a different pace. Some will jog while others will sprint. Some are great at marathons, while for others it takes all that they have to simply put one foot in front of the other year after year. The homeschooled children who win spelling bees and become doctors before they get their driver's licenses should be an encouragement to us. Rejoice in their success. We are all in the same race, just at a different pace.

Today's Prayer

Father, help us keep our eyes on the goal you have set for our families and not on the other runners. Help us to be sensitive to those families who may feel they are too far behind and may be tempted to give up the race.

Just for Today

Race with your children today! Try a three-legged race, an obstacle race, somersaults, or on your knees. Make sure everyone who finishes gets a reward.

SEVENTEEN

Bar Mitzvah

Behold, children are a gift of the Lord; the fruit of the womb is a reward.

PSALM 127:3

When my oldest child was just a newborn I remember thinking, *"I can't wait for her to be able to hold up her head."* Later on I thought, *"I can't wait for her to be able to sit by herself."* Once that was accomplished I envisioned the day when she would be able to crawl from room to room to find me, and then the day she would walk.

With each new accomplishment came an independence that changed our roles forever. As the years passed and she learned how to do more and more on her own, I found I had less to say about how she did her hair, the clothes she chose to wear, and what she ordered off the menu.

I saw these changes as good and healthy, important steps to help her become a mature adult. Yet I found it increasingly difficult to relate to her as a young woman. I could only see her as a child. Tensions surfaced on both sides, which caused us to cry out to the Lord for help.

In the Jewish tradition, thirteen-year-olds are ushered formally into adulthood with a special ceremony called a *bar mitzvah (bas mitzvah* for girls). The Lord led us to help our children make the transition into adulthood by having a sort of Christian *bar mitzvah* for each of them.

We spent the school year before the thirteenth birthday of each of our children teaching and reviewing all the doctrines of our faith. We gave them passages of Scripture to memorize and

41

talked extensively about what responsibilities they would have as adults.

As the big day approached, we sent invitations to family and friends to join us on the appointed Sunday afternoon. The ceremony included a time of reflection on our child's life up to that point, music, questioning on doctrinal issues, and finally the formal presentation of this former child as an adult.

After the cake was eaten and the gifts had been opened, our relationship with that child was never again the same. Nagging, corporal punishment, and childish things quickly became a part of the past. Responsibility, natural consequences, and maturity blossomed.

I discovered that the ceremony was just as important for my husband and me. We needed a point in time when we could begin to treat our children as adults. Doing this removed nearly all the tension and frustration from our relationships.

Today's Prayer

Dear Lord, thirteen years seem such a short time to have a "child." Help us make the best of those years and prepare our children to become mature, responsible adults.

Just for Today

Dig out baby pictures after dinner and have a walk down memory lane.

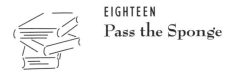

EIGHTEEN

Pass the Sponge

Let your light shine before men in such a way that they may see
your good works, and glorify your Father who is in heaven.

MATTHEW 5:16

I recently taught my young daughter Connie how to wipe down the bathroom counters using a sponge. Bless her heart. She worked so hard trying to get those counters clean, but when she was done someone had to go in after her and soak up all the water on the counter with a big towel. Her sponge always collected more liquid than her tiny hands could wring out. Until she grows big enough to wring out that sponge by herself, we have to mop up after her when she is done.

About the same time, on Sunday mornings we began to hear things like, "Do I have to go to church?" "Can't I stay home today?" "There's nothing to do!" Our first reaction was to wave the Bible over our children's heads and recite Scriptures that encourage church attendance. When the objections still came, we panicked, prayed, and tried to figure out why some were reluctant to go to church. After observing them through the following month of Sundays, we realized that our children's complaints were coming from what we now call the "full sponge syndrome."

Between homeschooling, devotions, Bible study, Sunday school, Vacation Bible School, and a host of other things, they were spiritually full. They had taken in principle after precept, but, like a sponge, they had not been wrung out. They were not being given opportunities to practice what they had been taught. They had no ministry or place of service. As a result they were spiritually restless, bored, and unproductive.

As we prayed about places of service for each of them, we began to notice opportunities both in the church and in our community. Soon our children were serving the Lord in the church by ushering, running the sound board, helping with the overheads, and working with the puppet ministry. Outside the church they got involved with the Red Cross, nursing homes, and community projects. The more they served, the more they looked forward to going to church. Opportunities to minister helped them wring out their spiritual sponges and created a thirst to know and experience God more.

Today's Prayer

Dear Lord, wring us out spiritually through a place of service and ministry, and then fill us with even more of you.

Just for Today

Have your children take some sponges, cut them into shapes like hearts and stars, dip them in paint, and blot them on paper to make "sponge art."

NINETEEN

God Bless the Gideons

And let us not lose heart in doing good, for in due time we shall reap if we do not grow weary.

GALATIANS 6:9

The new school year had just begun and I was already feeling like a failure. My ten-year-old son had been struggling to learn how to read. At the end of the last school year, he had just gotten his letters and sounds down pat. Now, days into the new school year, he had a discouraging battle with a reading lesson and cried out, "Oh, Mom, why do I have to read anyway?"

I opened my mouth to answer him but nothing came out. Instead the question vibrated and echoed through my brain. *Why did he have to learn to read?* As I thought through all the answers I should give him, only one seemed important enough to put him through such discouragement and despair.

"Honey," I began, "I want you to learn to read so that you will someday be able to read God's Word for yourself. Once you do, you will be better able to apply it to your life." Learning to read anything else would play second fiddle to the most important reason for reading. To have my son learn to read God's Word for himself became my prayer and goal for the school year.

For the next ten months we muddled through a systematic reading program and remained faithful to the task. In October we suspended seatwork for a week while we participated in some old-fashioned tent revival meetings. Faithfully at the door of the tent every night, a representative from the Gideon Bible

Society offered pocket Bibles to anyone who wanted one. My children were delighted, and each accepted one.

A couple of weeks after the revival had finished, my son excitedly called me into his room one night. "Mom, listen to this. It's really cool!" With that my reluctant reader found John 3:16 in his Gideon Bible and began to read. But he didn't stop with verse 16. He went on to read verse after verse—and all at once the Lord reminded me of my January prayer. All I could do was stand at his door and weep.

Today's Prayer

Dear Lord, never let us forget that you love our children even more than we do, and you want them to be able to read your Word. Thank you for the joy of seeing that happen.

Just for Today

Take time today and ask each of your reading children to read from one of their favorite books of the Bible.

TWENTY

Faithful

All these died in faith, without receiving the promises, but having seen them and having welcomed them from a distance, and having confessed that they were strangers and exiles on the earth.

HEBREWS 11:13

We began our radio ministry on Saturday, March 12, 1994. After four years of hard work and perseverance, our Saturday program was being carried by over one hundred affiliate radio stations. So we decided to launch a daily broadcast.

Two weeks into our daily broadcast schedule, we learned that a major network of stations had decided to cancel our program. In addition, a number of other stations had been sold or had changed formats, reducing our affiliates to seventy-seven for the weekend show and only seven for the daily. To make matters worse, none of the daily stations were able to air the broadcast live, so after four months of daily broadcasts we didn't have a single caller.

Finally one day the depression hit. *Why, Lord?* The time, energy, and finances it took to broadcast each day were staggering, and yet we were not seeing any visible signs of success. In tears, I shared my feelings with my husband.

Quoting Mother Teresa of Calcutta, Terry reminded me that "God hasn't called us to be successful. He's called us to be faithful."

What a powerful statement! He then read Hebrews 11 to me and showed me how Abel, Enoch, Noah, Abraham, and Sarah all lived by faith, looking forward to something that they never really attained on earth. In some cases it took thousands of years before the promises of God were realized.

The number of radio stations we were on, the advertisers, the sponsors, and all that measured earthly success were in the hands of the Lord, Terry reminded me. Our only responsibility was to be faithful, producing the best broadcast we could every day, no matter how many listeners we reached.

This lesson applied to my homeschooling as well. Was I more concerned about being successful or being faithful? The real success of what we are doing may be recognized only by future generations, long after we have gone to be with the Lord. Don't worry if no one notices your diligent effort now. You're in good company.

Today's Prayer

Dear Lord, thank you for the reminder that in everything we do, including homeschooling, if we are faithful then we are successful.

Just for Today

Write the phrase FAITHFUL = SUCCESSFUL on the top of a piece of paper, set the timer for five minutes, and see how many words of three or more letters you and your children can make.

TWENTY-ONE

Stressed Out

For if Abraham was justified by works, he has something to boast about; but not before God. For what does the Scripture say? And Abraham believed God, and it was reckoned to him as righteousness.

ROMANS 4:2-3

I woke up one morning with a smile on my face. This was to be the first full day of a new school schedule. I love the first day of school, and at first I couldn't wait to get going. Then I thought about all the other things I needed to do that day—meals to fix, a guest to interview for the radio broadcast, writing that needed to be done.

I pulled the pillow over my head and decided not to get out of bed after all. I felt my blood pressure rise under the stress of everything I needed to get done for the day. How could I do it all? How could I do any of it? And how well would any of it be done anyway?

Before I got out of bed I read Romans 4 and was reminded that, just like you and me, Abraham wasn't blessed because of what he *did* for God; he was blessed because of his *faith*. Abraham believed God would accomplish his will, and that he was invited to be a part of it. As I read, the Spirit of God reminded me that his will was going to be accomplished, with or without me. Yet, what a blessing it is to be a part of that plan!

God doesn't expect us to be "super moms," with super-human strength, intellect, or organizational skills. As a matter of fact, the fewer natural abilities we have, the more glory and honor he gets when we get things done right.

After thanking the Lord for the encouragement and direction he had given me for the day, I jumped out of bed and hit the floor running. All day long God continued to remind me through comments, verses, and circumstances to let him work through me.

As it turned out, it was the best homeschool start we had ever had. I didn't accomplish everything I had planned, but I found that as the day progressed, my schedule sort of naturally merged with what the Father had for me to do. No stress, no tears, and no regrets. Even my children commented on what a good day it had been.

Why can't every day be like that? Maybe it can.

Today's Prayer

O Father, we are so grateful that you use ordinary and sometimes even inadequate vessels like us to do your work. Thanks for the awesome privilege.

Just for Today

Plan to take a long, hot, destressing soak in a bubble bath tonight!

TWENTY-TWO
Quitting Time

I can do all things through Him who strengthens me.

PHILIPPIANS 4:13

Not too long ago, toward the end of a school year, our family experienced the "we'll only do our schoolwork when mom reminds us" syndrome. If I didn't crack the educational whip, the children would skip out of their seatwork. I was turning into a first-class nag. Pressure was mounting.

One day I had a series of meetings and appointments outside the home. Before I left I gave careful verbal and written instructions as to what schoolwork and chores had to be done that day.

I thoroughly enjoyed my day out, until I got home and discovered that no one had completed his or her assignments. Some hadn't even gotten a good start. They began the day by chopping and stacking wood, but of course there were breaks for tree climbing, volleyball, and bike riding.

"Look out! She's gonna blow!"

I did! Shame on me, but I blew my stack. I also delivered a fine speech about how education was a privilege and until they decided they wanted to be educated, I quit. You could have heard an apple drop!

While I pouted in my room, Dad and the kids had a family meeting. They all agreed that they needed to be more supportive and to take responsibility for their own learning habits. That evening we apologized to each other, and we started over the next day.

No matter what job, responsibility, or ministry the Lord

gives us, at some point we will grow weary and feel like giving up. When those days come, and they will, you may be tempted to throw up your hands and say, "I quit!" Yet, the same God who "gives us strength" also knows our limits, and since he has promised never to give us more than we can handle, it's really up to him to tell us when it's "quitting time." Hang in there!

Today's Prayer

Dear Lord, sometimes we do feel like quitting. Thank you for giving us the grace and encouragement to go on.

Just for Today

Quit! Declare a teacher holiday, pack a picnic lunch, and take off with your kids to the park. Just don't forget to come back tomorrow.

TWENTY-THREE

The Best Schedule

Now the people became like those who complain of adversity in the hearing of the Lord; and when the Lord heard it, His anger was kindled, and the fire of the Lord burned among them and consumed some of the outskirts of the camp.

NUMBERS 11:1

"Aw, do we have to do school today?"

What parent hasn't heard that phrase? It used to be heard frequently around our house as the first hints of summer turned the air warm. Some days my heart melted and I gave in to their cries for mercy. Soon, however, I discovered that, given an inch, they returned with a mile of moans the next day.

At the beginning of the following school year I surprised the children by handing them a beautiful new calendar. "The law says that you must be in school for 172 days this year. Here is a calendar containing 365 days. You decide which days you would like to have school. The only stipulations are that, first, you must all be in agreement on which days school will be in session and, second, I give final approval on days that may be in conflict with other events."

Talk about excitement! The children discussed the days and all agreed that Saturdays, Sundays, birthdays, and major holidays would be off. One by one they narrowed the list down and two hours later they proudly presented me with a finished school calendar. On the days selected for school a big "S" filled the box.

I must admit they were very creative in their selection process. I then took the calendar and wrote up a contract on the front. "We the undersigned students of the Brady Home School agree that we will do our schoolwork without complaint on the days marked with a red 'S.' All other days will be holidays. Work not completed on a school day will be finished on the next holiday."

Wearing huge smiles, all the children happily signed their names. The next time one of the children started complaining about having to do school on a warm, sunny day, I took him by the hand and showed him the calendar with the big "S." No more complaints!

The calendar worked well for the children, but it also helped me stick to the course. Sometimes my giving in to their pleas was as much for me as for them. Having the calendar gave us all the shot of discipline we needed.

Today's Prayer

Dear Lord, forgive us for all the complaining we do. Thank you for giving us creative solutions to difficult problems.

Just for Today

Flip through your school calendar and thank God for all the days you have had with your children.

TWENTY-FOUR

Worthy

I will give thanks to Thee, for I am fearfully and wonderfully made; wonderful are Thy works, and my soul knows it very well.
PSALM 139:14

During the year we lived in New Zealand, we were frequently visited by families who were interested in home-schooling and needed advice. Over one thousand people came through our door before we stopped counting.

One day a Maori family called and asked if they could come and talk. They were a lovely family with five delightful children. The eldest daughter was being promoted to the next grade level the following term, and the parents were anxious. She had never been a strong reader and was failing all her subjects in her current grade level.

After talking to the girl, it was clear that she had been taught to read by memorizing each word rather than by "sounding out" each letter. This method works for some children but not for most. Clearly this girl was part of the majority group.

In order to determine which grade level her reading fell into, I pulled out some books and put one in front of her. Since she should have been reading at an eighth-grade level, I chose a second-grade reader, thinking it would be good for her to succeed with that before progressing on to more difficult material.

A pained look crossed the girl's face. She stumbled through one or two sentences, getting most of the words wrong, before she burst into tears. She couldn't read. Her brothers and sisters gently put their arms around her and held her until the sobbing stopped.

"I'm so stupid," she said quietly as she wiped her eyes. Her whole self-worth was tied up in her ability to read. Now my eyes were wet. For hours I talked to her about different ways to learn, and then I began to teach her phonics. In a short period of time the light dawned. Once she knew a few simple sounds and saw how she could put these sounds together to make words, she was elated.

Rug, rag, rat, tar. The more she learned, the more she wanted to learn. Before she left that day she smiled and said, "I guess I'm not so stupid after all!"

That day I saw how vital it is for our children to see themselves as God sees them. It is important they learn that they are not valuable because of what they can do, but because of who they are.

Today's Prayer

Dear Lord, how many other children are going through life feeling defeated at such a young age? What can we do to help not only our own children but others as well?

Just for Today

Talk to your family about starting an after-school reading club for your neighborhood. You may find there are a few adults that want to join, too!

TWENTY-FIVE

Work It Out!

Like one who takes a dog by the ears is he who passes by and meddles with strife not belonging to him.

PROVERBS 26:17

Two of my boys were in a certain reading program, which required them to share one book. Every morning a fight erupted over who got to use the book first. Today was no different. After verbally sparring and arguing they came to me to mediate.

Usually I went through the whole routine of asking who had had the book first the day before, who was done with everything else, and so on and so forth, but not today.

"Work it out!" I told them.

I think my response startled them. They were used to Mom being the mediator and decision maker. Isn't that what moms do? I could see the wheels in their heads turning. *What does she mean, "Work it out"?*

After they thought about it for a few seconds one boy turned to the other. "Why don't we draw straws or have Mom pick a number between one and ten? Or maybe we could try a game of tic-tac-toe and the winner gets the book."

"Why not do all three?" came the response.

For the next ten minutes the boys did just that, agreeing that the best of three would win. I almost spoke up and put a stop to it, thinking it would just take away precious school time, but the Holy Spirit restrained me. This *was* precious school time!

After the winner was declared, they happily went about the rest of their schoolwork. I was amazed. No fighting, no yelling, and no "Mom!" They had actually worked through this problem without me. (Sometimes children will need a little more direction than just "work it out"—a list of suggestions or options, perhaps.)

That day was very enlightening for me. I began to think of other areas in which I might need to "let go" so that their problem-solving skills might get stronger.

As parents and teachers, we need to keep our children under control. Yet, in another sense we also need to be working ourselves out of a job. As our children take on more and more responsibility for problem solving, they need to experience our confidence in them and their ability to "work it out."

Today's Prayer

Dear Lord, thank you for the creativity you give our children. Thank you even for the problems they have and the solutions you provide.

Just for Today

When's the last time you played tic-tac-toe with your children? Why not today!

TWENTY-SIX

The Clique

Whoever is wise, let him understand these things; whoever is discerning, let him know them. For the ways of the Lord are right, and the righteous will walk in them, but transgressors will stumble in them.

HOSEA 14:9

Years ago, when homeschooling was just beginning to catch on, the Lord moved us to a new town and church. Several families, sensing God's leading, began to homeschool and were very successful.

About a year later another mother in the church came to me and asked if I would help her get started as well. This woman had three boys who desperately wanted their mother's attention and would sometimes do foolish things to get it.

I had noticed that the mother, too, seemed to crave the acceptance and friendship of the other ladies in church. I hoped this wasn't her reason for wanting to homeschool—it can be challenging enough for those who believe it is what the Lord is calling them to do. Finally, however, I realized it wasn't my job to assess her motivation, and agreed to help her. I really hoped homeschooling would awaken her to the beautiful treasures she had in her sons.

On Sunday after her first week of school she sought me out and gave me a full report. Her concluding remark was, "Well, I guess this makes me part of the clique!" This dear mother tried to homeschool for almost another two years before she finally gave up and put the boys back in school.

I wish I could tell you that homeschooling saved this

woman's life and that she and her family lived happily ever after, but I can't. The experience was a disaster for both her and her family. It nearly destroyed her marriage, and it deepened the chasm that had already begun to form between her and her children.

Homeschooling is not some "lucky charm" or magical solution to life's disappointments. It is hard work, and keeps you on your knees before God. Even so, I have seen families who began to homeschool for all the wrong reasons succeed as they have discovered the many unexpected blessings and benefits of this important ministry.

Homeschooling is not just about education. It is about obedience, learning how to hear the voice of the Lord, and walking in his ways. It is like anything else we do in life. It should be done because the Lord calls us to it and for his honor and glory.

Today's Prayer

Dear Lord, search our hearts. Are we homeschooling for the right reasons?

Just for Today

Recall the day you knew the Lord wanted you to homeschool. Write it down along with any verses of Scripture that he gave you to confirm it.

TWENTY-SEVEN

The Final Chapter

"For I know the plans that I have for you," declares the Lord, "plans for welfare and not for calamity to give you a future and a hope."

JEREMIAH 29:11

"Mr. and Mrs. Brady, I hate to be the one to tell you this, but the brain insult your daughter suffered has left her with severe learning disabilities."

The doctor tried to be as gentle as possible, but the impact of his words left us breathless. Our six-month-old daughter's illness had rendered her incapable of learning like other children. For weeks we cried, thought of the "if onlys," and questioned why God would have let this happen.

In those early days, I felt the story of our lives would be one of despair and disappointment. Then we were introduced to homeschooling by another family whose "slow learner" had gone on to graduate with both a bachelor's and a master's degree. Our daughter could learn, but it was going to take a lot of time and patience, trial and error.

One day as I was reading the verse above, the past twenty-two years flashed before my eyes. I saw how during that time God had gradually revealed his plan for us, and that it was a good plan. What we had thought was a disaster became the hope for our future.

The Lord used our daughter's illness to teach us life lessons that could not have been learned otherwise. It drew us closer to him, led us to homeschool, trained us to help others, directed us to New Zealand as missionaries, inspired us to begin the radio ministry, and finally gave me the privilege of writing this devotional.

Through all of this I have gotten to know my wonderful heavenly Father better, and have learned to trust him when all seems hopeless. Whatever circumstances come into my life, I know he is in control and has a plan and a purpose. This includes big things, like illnesses and homeschooling decisions, as well as little things, like interruptions and test scores.

All the circumstances of our lives, good and bad, have been perfectly woven together into a unique manuscript. Remember, when you are tempted to despair, the last chapter of your book is yet to be written.

Today's Prayer

Dear Heavenly Father, thank you for allowing our pasts and for preparing our futures. Thank you for hope.

Just for Today

Read or tell the story of Joseph to your children. See how he trusted God under the most unfair and hopeless circumstances—even while in an Egyptian prison!

TWENTY-EIGHT

Our Worst Fears

Then he answered and said to me, "This is the word of the Lord to Zerubbabel saying, Not by might nor by power, but by My Spirit says the Lord of hosts."

ZECHARIAH 4:6

One day a homeschool support group visited our studios, took the grand tour, and ended up on our broadcast. Six students and two moms took turns being on the radio; they had a blast and did a great job.

While interviewing each of the students, I discovered that all had been in public and private schools before being home schooled. Most had only been homeschooling for the past six to eighteen months. When I asked them what had most concerned them about the idea of being homeschooled, they all had one common fear. They were sure that homeschooling meant the end of their social lives, and that they would lose all of their friends.

Did their "worst fear" come to pass? The answer was a unanimous "no!" They discovered that their old friends were still there, and now they had new ones through support group field trips.

The interview reminded me of what my own homeschooling fears had been. I've heard these same concerns expressed by other parents as well: *What if my children do not learn? Will they fall behind other children? Can I afford the books? What will my friends think? How will my family respond? Will Social Services take my children? Will my children be able to go to college? Will they know how to play with other children? What if I don't understand the books? What if they want to learn calculus?*

Each time one of these fears surfaces, I like to picture the Son and the Father having a conversation in heaven.

"Father, you've called this family to homeschool, but there seem to be problems. I don't think the mom is qualified—her children will end up way behind, unable to catch up. Maybe they'll wind up in a foster home."

"Son, you're right. There's another snag, too. I forgot to arrange for the financing, so they will have to wing it without books. By the way, did you prepare their friends and family for this decision?"

"Me? I thought you covered that!"

When I imagine this heavenly conversation, it always puts a smile on my face. God knew exactly what he was doing when he called us to homeschool our children. Fear not, because our human strength will have nothing to do with our success. Success will come by his Spirit.

Today's Prayer

Dear Lord, thank you for the power of your Spirit and all it will accomplish in our homeschooling homes.

Just for Today

Have a good old-fashioned arm wrestling contest with your children. Remind them of the difference between our power and God's power.

TWENTY-NINE

God Knows

For by Him all things were created, both in the heavens and on earth, visible and invisible, whether thrones or dominions or rulers or authorities—all things have been created by Him and for Him.

COLOSSIANS 1:16

Most children will lie at least once in their life—though some are not as good at it as others. Thankfully, this was the case with one of my girls. She rarely even tried to deceive us.

Then one day a situation came up where she insisted she hadn't committed a particular offense, though I was fairly certain that she had. Her story was believable, but after a quick prayer for discernment I felt she had sinned and lied about it, so I disciplined her accordingly.

After we had prayed together, she cuddled on my lap. "Mommy," she asked thoughtfully, "how did you know?"

"Well," I explained, "ever since you accepted Jesus as your personal Savior, you have had the Holy Spirit living in you. I have the Holy Spirit living in me, too, so he will give me wisdom and understanding when I need to know something. He helped me to see that you weren't telling the truth so that I could help you learn to do what is right in the future."

My daughter thought this over for a few minutes and responded, "Mom, I'm not so sure I want to have the Holy Spirit living in me if he's going to tattle on me all the time!"

Years later, I still chuckle when I remember that exchange. However, recently the Lord used that memory to show me even greater spiritual implications. Since God is the Creator of everything, he knows all there is to know about this world. And with his Spirit living in me and in my saved children, we all have access to the very foundation of all truth and learning.

Understanding this concept took away the fear I had of teaching about satellites, calculus, the Pythagorean theorem, and even deep spiritual truth. If we come across something we do not understand, we can go to the Lord and ask him for wisdom. He will lead us to the source of the knowledge we need. Count on it!

Today's Prayer
Dear Lord, thank you for the Holy Spirit who cares enough to tell us when we are wrong and loves enough to lead us to all truth.

Just for Today
Have your children bake a cake by asking you about each step instead of using a recipe. Demonstrate how you can lead them through the process, just as the Lord can lead us no matter what situation we are in.

THIRTY

High Anxiety

Be anxious for nothing, but in everything by prayer and suppli-cation with thanksgiving let your requests be made known to God.
PHILIPPIANS 4:6

I was literally biting my nails. The boys were about to take their first standardized achievement test, and I was a bundle of nerves. Memories of all the broadcasts I had ever done on testing flashed through my mind—which only made matters worse.

All the programs had two things in common. First, the experts said not to worry about these tests. Second, we were reminded that these kinds of tests fail to measure the really important aspects of our children's education, such as character, honesty, and compassion. For years I had encouraged listeners not to worry, to relax and enjoy the testing experience. Now I was doing just the opposite. That only added to my nail biting.

I was able to observe my sons during the test, which increased my anxiety. As I watched them choose the wrongly spelled word over the right one, every ounce of my being wanted to nudge their hand to the correct answer. I desperately wanted to shake my head yes as they vacillated between two choices and widely grin as they neared the right solution to a math problem. (I didn't, of course.)

At times I watched in horror as they had to guess at questions we had not even covered in school, making me feel all the more like a failure. By the time they finished their first standardized achievement test, I was exhausted.

When the results came back, my sons' scores averaged in the seventieth and eightieth percentiles. So why had I been so anxious? In my own mind, their scores were a measurement not only of their own academic achievement but of my own teaching and ministry as well. What if they had done poorly? Could I continue to teach them if it wasn't working? And if I didn't homeschool, how could I continue my radio broadcast or write books?

When God says not to "be anxious," it is not a suggestion, it is a command. My anxiety had no effect on their test scores. According to medical research, it probably raised my blood pressure and cholesterol levels. So why worry?

Today's Prayer

Heavenly Father, sometimes we get anxious about the silliest things. Help us take your command to be anxious for nothing, and take everything to you in prayer.

Just for Today

Take a notebook and label it "Casting Cares." Inside, write down each of the things that you are anxious about and then pray and ask God to take care of them. Come back next week with your new cares and see how God has answered your prayers and relieved you of your anxiety.

THIRTY-ONE

Precious Versus Worthless

Therefore, thus says the Lord, if you return, then I will restore you—Before Me you will stand; and if you extract the precious from the worthless, you will become My spokesman. They for their part may turn to you, but as for you, you must not turn to them.

JEREMIAH 15:19

Every year on December thirty-first, my husband shares with the family our "New Year Charge": goals and direction that he believes the Lord has given us for the new year. Each member of the family is given special Scripture verses to memorize and apply to his or her life.

This special time of family sharing is exciting, and it often ends up being prophetic. We are always in awe at how often the Lord changes us in the very areas my husband had predicted the year before.

This year the phrase "separate the precious from the worthless" has been on the tips of all of our tongues and written on our hearts. Each day I find myself examining the content of what I am teaching my children. Is it precious? Does it edify their spirits and minds? Or it is simply "busy work," a useless waste of time?

What about the words we speak to one another? Are they precious? Do they build others up, encourage them, and give them hope? Or are they worthless—cutting, discouraging, and defeating?

What about our recreation time? Is it being filled with the precious or the worthless? Have the many gifts God has entrusted to us been put to their best possible use?

Scripture tells us that "the ordinances of the Lord are sure and altogether righteous; they are more precious than gold" (Ps 19:9b-10). The value of each action, each word, each thought, must be determined by the holy standard of God's Word. To the extent that we embrace its teachings, our lives will reflect the precious light and life of God.

Today's Prayer

My Heavenly Father, help us separate the precious from the worthless today in everything we do, speak, and think.

Just for Today

Slip a precious coin in one pocket and a worthless rock in the other. When one of your children says or does something precious, give them the coin to carry for awhile. When their actions or speech are worthless, remind them by producing the worthless rock from your pocket. Perhaps the whole family can pass the two among them for the day and see how many times each one ends up carrying the precious coin.

THIRTY-TWO
One at a Time

Now while Ezra was praying and making confession, weeping and prostrating himself before the house of God, a very large assembly, men, women, and children, gathered to him from Israel; for the people wept bitterly.

EZRA 10:1

After Israel's seventy years of captivity, God fulfilled the promise he had made to them through Jeremiah to bring his people back to their land. Ezra, a scribe, was used by God to reacquaint the Jews with the Book of the Law. Once the reading of the Law took place, the Spirit of God convicted the people of their sin and a great revival broke out. While Ezra prostrated himself before the house of God, men, women, and children gathered and wept as they repented of their sin (see Ezr 10:1).

Dennis Rainey, host of "Family Life Today," tells us that great civilizations are destroyed and rebuilt the same way—one family at a time. If God gets a hold on your family and mine, that's two. If he is able to reach our children with the message of righteousness, purity, and courage, then look at how the message is multiplied.

Political issues have had a way of riling me up like nothing else could. There were times when I couldn't sleep at night for thinking about the legislation being passed that would endanger the family and ultimately our country. I would call, fax, e-mail everyone I could think of concerning issues like partial birth abortions and the U.N. Convention on the Rights of the Child.

One day the Lord helped me to find peace. He reminded me that Ezra had done what God called him to do. He looked at himself and repented. He took personal responsibility for his right relationship with God, then publicly went about God's business. Lying prostrate before God, Ezra was joined by another, and another. Soon the whole country was on its face before God.

I see the same thing happening within the homeschooling movement. Where there used to be five homeschool support groups for a whole state, now we have that many in just one city. Whole families are lying prostrate before God, weeping for their sin and doing what they can to raise a new generation to serve him.

Today's Prayer

O Father God, thank you for the work you are doing among families as they seek you above all else. We look forward to seeing what you will do with a new generation of dedicated believers.

Just for Today

Form a human pyramid, with Mom and Dad on their hands and knees, taking the bottom row. Then build from there.

THIRTY-THREE

King of the Hill

But now you also, put them all aside: anger, wrath, malice, slander, and abusive speech from your mouth.

COLOSSIANS 3:8

Finding flat land in the mountains is difficult; sometimes you have to make your own. We were having dirt hauled in from a building project in town to be used to expand a parking area just below our house. As the trucks dumped huge piles of dirt, my children raced to get their schoolwork done so they could go down and play King of the Hill.

One day as two of my sons pushed and shoved their way to the top of the hill, their playing got out of hand. Tempers flared, words were exchanged, and finally one boy was pushed down hard. As he landed, his hand hit a jagged boulder, and the next thing they knew there was blood everywhere.

Given the option of stitches and a small scar or butterfly bandages and possibly a larger scar, my son opted for the bandages. We carefully dressed his wound, and once he was resting comfortably on the couch, we began to address an even more serious wound—his brother's heart. The uninjured boy felt worse than awful. He had pushed his brother in anger, and he sobbed to think of how his temper had inflicted such pain and suffering. We prayed with both of the boys and helped them to work through a very hurtful situation.

The next day we realized we had another problem. How was my young son supposed to do his schoolwork with his bandaged writing hand? From the looks of things he would be out of school for a week or so. As we discussed the problem, a very contrite son volunteered to write out his brother's lessons.

He had thought about it and had come up with a plan. His brother could read his own books, but when it came time to answer questions in his workbook or math book, he would give the answers orally. As my son laid out his plan I watched his eyes. He was excited and energized by the idea of being able to somehow make things up to his brother.

For a whole week he served his brother, until he was no longer needed. The math and reading lessons of the week have long been forgotten, but the lesson of putting away anger will last a lifetime.

Today's Prayer
Dear Lord, thank you for the healing, both in the hand and in the heart.

Just for Today
Find a place to play King of the Hill. Just watch out for sharp, jagged rocks!

THIRTY-FOUR
Socialization

Now we command you, brethren, in the name of our Lord Jesus Christ, that you keep aloof from every brother who leads an unruly life and not according to the tradition which you received from us.

2 THESSALONIANS 3:6

After a series of articles on homeschooling came out in major newsmagazines, I was asked to do interviews on radio stations around the country. As the interviews came, the questions were often predictable. Usually the first—and never later than the second—question out of the interviewer's mouth was, "Won't homeschooled children have trouble fitting in if they aren't around other children all day?"

I would explain that by homeschooling my children I was able to carefully pick and choose the socialization my children were getting. Socialization does not mean we are to dump our children into a room with children the same age who have ungodly standards, morals, and vocabularies, and just hope for the best.

One interviewer suggested that by not being placed in that environment, my children would become racist. I explained that God's standard for whom we are to socialize with has nothing to do with social or economic background, race, physical appearance, or handicaps.

God's standard for choosing our friends is clear. In 1 Corinthians 15:33 we are told, "Do not be deceived: bad company corrupts good morals." This doesn't mean that all our children's friends must be saved—or even that they should be allowed to play with any Christian family. Some of the worst language my children ever heard came from the mouths of kids from Christian families!

Select carefully those with whom your children are allowed to socialize. Does this rule out any unsaved relationships in our children's lives? Absolutely not! When the unsaved children come to play, we simply beef up our parenting and monitoring.

Most children will do what is right as long as an adult is within earshot or eyeshot. Yet if they are not allowed to play with your kids, how else will these unchurched little ones have an opportunity to see Christianity at work? When they play at your house, they play by your rules. In a school setting, godly rules are usually not applied, and in that case, everyone loses.

Today's Prayer

Dear Lord, thank you for the unsaved families and friends you have brought into our lives. Help us to be a living testimony of Jesus Christ before them, that they might see and believe.

Just for Today

Make a list of all the unsaved children in your life. Pray for them and make plans to have them over for several visits throughout the year.

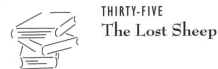

THIRTY-FIVE

The Lost Sheep

*But may it never be that I should boast, except in the cross of our
Lord Jesus Christ, through which the world has been crucified to
me, and I to the world.*

GALATIANS 6:14

One morning as I sat across the table from one home-schooling mother, I prayed as tears streamed down her face. One of her children had totally turned her back on the Lord. Her daughter had moved out of the house, started drinking, and recently announced that she was taking a female partner.

"Where have I failed?" this woman sobbed. "If only I had started sooner."

This woman and her husband had surrendered to the Lord when their children were very little. Although they had not grown up in Christian homes themselves, they had become strong in their beliefs and were consistent, godly parents. She feared that not knowing the Lord herself until she was in her early thirties had somehow contributed to her daughter's rebellion.

"How are your other children handling this?" I inquired. She said that two of the others were still in Bible college, the oldest daughter was now married to a youth pastor, and her youngest would be graduating from their homeschool in the spring and heading off on a youth missionary project to Central America.

"Your other four are doing very well," I commented.

"Oh, that's not because of anything I've done," she replied.

"The Lord gets all the glory for those four. He is the one who saved them, helped me homeschool them, and called them into his service."

"Why, then," I inquired, "are you taking the blame for your one child who has chosen not to follow the Lord?"

As parents, we do the best we can. Our children have free wills and can choose to follow the Lord or not. Just as we cannot take the credit when they choose to follow him, we cannot take the blame when they don't.

Some parents do everything right and see their children fall away. Others do everything wrong and yet their children become vibrant, committed Christians. Choosing to follow the Lord is something that our children do, not because of us, but because the Spirit of the Lord draws them. Even so, we have a responsibility to live Christ before our children, to pray for them, and to introduce them to spiritual truth. But remember: the outcome is the Lord's.

Today's Prayer

Dear Lord, thank you for the privilege of parenthood. Help us to do the best we can and to trust you for the results.

Just for Today

Read the story of the Prodigal Son found in Luke 15:11. Act it out together or with puppets.

THIRTY-SIX

Practical Application

He has told you, O man, what is good; and what does the Lord re-
quire of you but to do justice, to love kindness, and to walk humbly
with your God?

MICAH 6:8

After one of our broadcasts, a father called from Kansas to say he wanted to homeschool immediately. The decision to homeschool came as a result of a trip to the grocery store. His two daughters went with him, and he asked them to compare the prices on two cans of tomatoes and give him the one with the best value.

The junior high girls looked at him as though he were speaking some foreign language. He carefully explained how to figure the cost per ounce, and still the girls didn't get it. Before they got to the checkout line, he asked the girls to estimate the cost of the ten items in his cart and round off the total to the nearest dollar.

The girls were lost, and the father was hot. He had been sending them to a private school, where they were receiving straight As in math, yet they could not practically apply any of the concepts they were learning in school to real life.

I am seeing the same parallel in our children with regard to their spiritual lives. Parents are buying expensive Bible curriculums, sending their children to Sunday school and church, and yet these children are not able to apply biblical concepts to their everyday lives.

They can tell us how many missionary trips Paul took, what sandals he wore, and what he ate along the way, but they cannot share their faith with their friends down the street. Some cannot apply the principles of God's Word to fights they are having with their brothers and sisters, and don't know what it means to honor their father and mother.

One way we can encourage our children to apply the Bible to everyday situations is to take verses of Scripture, explain and memorize them, and then ask our children to identify hypothetical situations to which the verses might apply: an argument at the breakfast table, taking a meal to a sick neighbor, or unfinished schoolwork.

Knowing things about God and the Bible is nice—but knowing God himself, understanding his ways, and being able to apply Scripture to our everyday lives need to be the real goals.

Today's Prayer

Dear Lord, keep us from pressing for an outward performance without an inward change of heart. Help our children to really get to know you today.

Just for Today

Memorize a Bible verse. Ask your children to role-play a situation where they could apply this verse to a problem or a blessing.

THIRTY-SEVEN

The Greatest Goal

*For the eyes of the Lord search back and forth across the whole
earth, looking for people whose hearts are perfect toward Him, so
that He can show His great power in helping them.*

2 CHRONICLES 16:9a, TLB

A wise person once said, "If you aim at nothing, you'll hit
it every time." Society tells us that the ultimate goals are
to acquire money, power, or fame. How does the way we live
reflect our goals and priorities as Christian parents?

Many years ago, while sitting in a church service, my husband and I heard a missionary to Asia talk about the great
things the Lord was doing there. He took no credit for the
miraculous things going on, but simply quoted 2 Chronicles
16:9 and challenged each of us to take this verse to heart. My
husband reached for my hand, and together we set this verse as
the ultimate goal for our lives.

There have been times when we have struggled to have a
heart totally turned toward him and have been tempted to
slack off. But each time, the Lord has reminded us of this verse
and encouraged us to keep going. From time to time we are
reminded of areas in our hearts that are turned toward our own
way and need a midcourse correction. Yet as we have made
those adjustments, we have experienced God's support and
have seen his power working though us. Once you have had a
taste of that, you'll settle for nothing less.

Our children need opportunities to make this same kind of
commitment for themselves. To accomplish this we need to
teach them not only reading, writing, and arithmetic, but of

men and women like David, Daniel, Esther, Deborah, Abraham, and Moses. The examples of these men and women show our children how God can work through a heart that is totally turned toward him.

Our children can and should have an ultimate goal that is not money, power, or fame. They need to know that the greatest goal is to have a heart turned toward God. No matter what ministry God calls them to, they need to experience the power of God in their lives firsthand.

Today's Prayer

Dear Lord, thank you for all that you are doing to conform us and turn our hearts toward you. Help us to keep that goal before our children.

Just for Today

Even if it is not Valentine's Day, cut out some red paper hearts and print words on them like "thoughts, attitudes, actions." Take those hearts and place them on a brown paper cross. Help your children to see how it is that we turn our hearts toward him.

THIRTY-EIGHT

Holy Discontent

I urge you therefore, brethren, by the mercies of God, to present your bodies as a living and holy sacrifice, acceptable to God, which is your spiritual service of worship. And do not be conformed to this world, but be transformed by the renewing of your mind, that you may prove what the will of God is, that which is good and acceptable and perfect.

ROMANS 12:1-2

At one of our homeschool family camps we met with a group of about a dozen homeschooling couples. As we talked, it became apparent that a number of these people were having difficulty in their churches.

"It's hard to find a church where we feel comfortable."

"We used to like our church ... but ever since we started homeschooling, it's like we just don't fit in anymore."

"There are so many 'surface Christians' in churches these days—it's hard to tell them apart from unbelievers. That goes for their kids, too. They spend hours on violent computer games—and the language! It's hard to find real fellowship."

In most cases, these homeschoolers had assumed the problem was theirs. Perhaps they were too picky, or too rebellious, or too proud. None of them could understand the uneasiness and depression they were feeling. We didn't know how to explain it, either. All we could do was encourage them and pray with them.

On one of our recent broadcasts we interviewed a pastor who was able to explain what in many cases is the root cause of these feelings. He spoke of the great revivals going on around the world and of the "holy discontent" that frequently characterizes an approaching movement of the Spirit. This "holy discontent," he explained, is common among many homeschooling families, whose dissatisfaction with the moral direction of schools causes them to take a careful look at their churches as well. Sadly, their pursuit of holiness and commitment to Scripture is not always shared or even understood by other Christians. As a result, many homeschooling families frequently feel ostracized and rejected in their own home churches. They are told to stop rocking the boat, and are lumped together as "legalistic homeschool radicals."

Feeling a "holy discontent" is not a shameful thing; it is what is natural when the Spirit of God draws you closer and closer to him. May we never get so comfortable with the way things are that we lose our holy discontent.

Today's Prayer

Dear Lord, thank you for the persecution and suffering we experience when we want more of you.

Just for Today

Pray with your children for your church and church leaders.

THIRTY-NINE

The Pain of the Past

The name of the Lord is a strong tower; the righteous runs into it and is safe.

PROVERBS 18:10

One of my favorite people to interview is Jackie Kendall, whose sense of humor and quick wit keep me in stitches. You wouldn't know it to look at her, but Jackie grew up in a dysfunctional home with an abusive father. She accepted Jesus Christ at a youth meeting as a teenager and went on to become an author, speaker, and president of Power to Grow Ministries.

After one interview we sat around sharing childhood memories. She told me about her father, and I told her about the orphanage in which I grew up. Back and forth we went, playing "top that pain." Then we each discussed how differently our children were growing up. They were thriving in Christian homes, being homeschooled, and living in environments of peace and safety.

"How I hope and pray my children will not have to endure the hurt we did as children," I commented to Jackie. She looked at me and said, "But Vicki, it was our pain that led us to Jesus."

She was right. Every one of us has tales of hurt, betrayal, and rejection that God has used to lead us to the love of Jesus Christ and a new life in him. Suffering is a part of life from which none of us are exempt.

As a parent I find myself trying hard to clear a path for my children, to keep them from any stones or gullies that might hurt them. Sometimes my time would be better spent teaching them how to handle the conflicts when they do come, and holding their hands while they heal. Avoiding needless pain and suffering is always good. Yet, we have to face facts: as long as there is breath in our children's bodies, they will suffer disappointment and loss.

There are even going to be times when our children will suffer because of mistakes we have made as parents. How many times have I had to apologize to my children and watch them suffer because of an unkind word or action on my part? But it is the suffering and hurt that gives them the opportunity to develop a love and a trust for Jesus Christ. Jesus is the only one who is completely dependable and will never let them down. As Jackie said to me at the close of our interview, "Vicki, we will never be such great parents that our children won't have a need for Jesus Christ."

Today's Prayer

Dear Lord, thank you for the hurt and pain of the past. Without it we never would have looked for a future, or found it in you.

Just for Today

Tell your children about how you came to know Jesus Christ as your personal Savior.

FORTY

Open Ears

I have no greater joy than this, to hear of my children walking in the truth.

3 JOHN 1:4

Some of the most important lessons our children ever learn are not received in a formal classroom situation. In some cases, we may not even be aware that "class is in session."

Not long ago, for example, we took part in a week-long tent revival that took place in our small community. For six days and nights preachers came, people were saved, and lives were changed. My children were there through the whole event, and by Thursday night we were all tired. That night my three girls, ages three, five, and seven, were allowed to color on paper toward the back of the tent while the service went on.

In the middle of the preaching I began to think about keeping them home the next night. After all, how much were they really absorbing while they colored? Maybe they needed their sleep more. About that time the fiery preacher asked a rhetorical question.

"Just who are you going to trust your future to?" he blasted through the microphone. Just then my seven-year-old, Helen, without looking up from her crayons and paper, whispered, "Jesus Christ." She *had* been listening. Message received, Lord!

Another example of what open ears can do came from my three-year-old, Anna. I would have her come into our classroom during Bible time, but did not expect her to participate or repeat the memory verses. I felt that exposing her to what was going on was important. At the end of the week I would have each of the children recite their memory verse and earn a special reward. One week's verse was John 15:5:

I am the vine, you are the branches. If a man remains in me and I in him he will bear much fruit. Apart from me you can do nothing.

The reward that week was chocolate kisses! After everyone had said the verse, I started to get into the rest of the day's work. Just then, little Anna stood up and said, "But Mommy, what about me? I want to do the verse too." In her three-year-old voice she recited:

I am the wine. You are the bwanches.
If a man remains in me and I in him
he will bury much fruit!
A part from me you can do 'nuffin.

Never underestimate the potential of open ears!

Today's Prayer
Dear Lord, thank you for ears that never close.

Just for Today
Take your children on a nature walk today. See how many sounds they can identify as they walk.

FORTY-ONE

Doctor for the Sick

And hearing this, Jesus said to them, "It is not those who are healthy who need a physician, but those who are sick; I did not come to call the righteous, but sinners."

MARK 2:17

From the moment Mary walked into the homeschool support group it was evident that she was not "one of them." Her outdated clothes reeked of stale cigarette smoke, and her preteen daughter was a moody girl with blue hair and earrings in places no one suspected earrings could be.

Mary and her daughter Megan stayed through the meeting, Mary raising her hand and asking what seemed to be one hundred questions. She had seen an announcement in her local paper advertising the homeschool support group meeting, and had thought that maybe this could be the answer to her problems with her daughter.

Megan had done fine in school until the previous year, when it became apparent that she was no longer a little girl. Now boys had become her only homework assignment. Her grades had dropped, her attendance had slipped, and the arguments with her mom had heated up. Life at home was becoming impossible, and her mother was desperate.

Only some of Mary's questions were answered that night, not nearly enough to give her the confidence she needed to get a good start. What about the state laws? How could Megan get a diploma? The support group leader spoke of a field trip to an ice cream factory. Maybe this was the way to begin?

The field trip was chilly, but not because of the ice cream.

Other than a few short "hellos," not one parent or child spoke to Mary or Megan—other than the rude little boy who told Megan that the ring through her nose made her look like a bull. Maybe homeschooling was not what Mary had thought it was going to be.

Mary tried hard to homeschool Megan and attended as many support group meetings as she could before she lost hope and gave up. Although she never knew about the phone calls group members made among themselves, expressing concern about how Megan might wrongly influence their children into ways of the world, Mary knew she wasn't welcome.

A short time later Megan quit school altogether, started doing drugs, and moved in with her latest boyfriend.

Jesus was criticized by the religious elite for reaching out to the outcasts and the socially sick, but he knew they were the ones who needed him the most. Are we following his example?

Today's Prayer

O Lord, show us how to use our homeschooling to reach out to the Marys and Megans of our communities, and give us hearts of compassion for them.

Just for Today

Pray for a neighbor, a relative, or a friend who has a child not walking with the Lord.

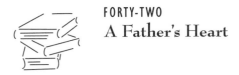

FORTY-TWO
A Father's Heart

And he will restore the hearts of the fathers to their children, and the hearts of the children to their fathers, lest I come and smite the land with a curse.

MALACHI 4:6

One night after a long school day, Dad offered to spring for pizza. At the time we were living in Arizona near an army base, so pizza carryouts were mighty popular. We called and placed our order, and at the appropriate time Dad went to pick up the pizza. He was gone for only about fifteen minutes, but when he came back I noticed emotion written all over his face. His eyes were moist.

I quickly looked for our young son, who had gone with his father. He was right next to Dad, with a bright smile on his face, stomping across the floor in his shiny new cowboy boots. What could possibly have happened? As Terry put the pizza down he told me the following story.

As he and three-year-old James went to pick up the pizza, James begged Dad to let him carry something. He insisted he could help with the drinks. Since Terry's hands were full, he agreed to let James carry one of the Cokes as they headed out of the packed restaurant lobby. As James reached the door, the heel of his new boot got caught on the threshold. Down he went, spilling Coke all over the lobby floor and on anyone close enough to see it splatter.

James looked up at his dad, tears brimming in his eyes. "I'm sorry, Daddy," he whispered. Terry put the pizza down and helped James up, asking him if he was all right. "I'm OK,

Daddy, but what about the Coke?"

"You're more important than that Coke," Terry replied, and together they mopped up the mess and apologized to the people who had been splashed. As Terry opened the door of the van to get in he felt a large hand on his shoulder. He turned to see the tallest army colonel he had ever seen in his life.

With tears in his eyes the colonel said, "Mister, I saw what happened with your boy back there. It's been a long time since I saw such love between a dad and his son. Most dads would have cussed their kid out or slapped him. Sir, I'd like to shake the hand of a real man and tell you to keep on doing what you're doing."

That day we realized that it is not only our children who are watching the things we do. Other people are watching, too—sometimes when we least expect it. What a responsibility!

Today's Prayer
Dear Lord, thank you for turning the hearts of the fathers to their children.

Just for Today
Make Dad's favorite dessert for dinner.

FORTY-THREE

Contentment

Not that I speak from want; for I have learned to be content in whatever circumstances I am.

PHILIPPIANS 4:11

Once a year I knew I could expect a phone call from a dear homeschooling mother in Colorado. She began to homeschool when her children were in the third and fifth grades, and each year she tried a new curriculum. Every year this mother would carefully evaluate the children's needs, verify her budget, quiz me about potential programs, and select materials that she thought were best for her children. Within six weeks after school began the children would begin to complain about the material, and they would whine their way through the whole school year.

This year when she called and asked to get together there was something different in her voice. We met for coffee, and I saw that she was happy and not stressed. After a few minutes of pleasant chitchat I asked her how I could help her with school this year. A huge smile stretched across her face as she exclaimed, "I won't be needing your help this year. It's all taken care of."

She went on to explain that, after praying and discussing the situation with her husband, she had taken her children down to the city homeschool bookstore. There she gave them a list of subjects they needed to cover for the school year, a spending limit, and the following instructions: "I will be back in two hours. Based on the guidelines I've given you, you have two hours to pick out your schoolwork for the next year. Bye-bye!"

When she returned two hours later she discovered that the children had picked out all their school materials, and had enough money left over for the family to go out for pizza.

Once she was home, she looked through the books and was amazed at what they had selected. In most cases they had picked out material that she would have thought far too difficult for them to handle. They didn't even wait for school to officially start the next week. After dinner they dug right in.

Three months of the school year went by before one of the children issued a complaint about the books. The mom simply smiled and said, "You picked them." She didn't need to say anything more.

Today's Prayer

Dear Heavenly Father, thank you for the books, materials, supplies, and creativity you give to us each and every year.

Just for Today

Offer a praise prayer for the many writers and publishers of homeschooling material.

FORTY-FOUR

The History Scroll

But if any of you lacks wisdom, let him ask of God, who gives to all men generously and without reproach, and it will be given to him.

JAMES 1:5

History was not my favorite subject when I was growing up, and I wanted to find an interesting way to teach it to my own children. I bought a couple of history books but could see my children zoning out, just as I once had.

I considered asking the Lord for wisdom, but figured that the wisdom God promised to give was for "spiritual" things, not everyday things like how to teach history. Later in the day when I was again fumbling through history, the Lord brought today's verse to mind. I stopped right there and asked God for wisdom in teaching this subject. After prayer I sensed the Lord asking me, "How did I teach history?"

How did the Lord teach history? When you look at the Bible, he taught history through biographies. In Genesis we learn all about creation, the flood, and the beginning of the Jewish nation through the life stories of Adam, Eve, Noah, and Abraham. It was then that the Lord gave me the idea for a history scroll.

I took about forty feet of butcher-block paper and attached a dowel rod to it at each end with staples. I made a "time line" across the paper, and marked off every inch to represent five-year intervals. When I got to the year 1900, every inch represented one year instead of five.

Once the scroll was finished, I read the biography of Joan of

Arc to the children. We located on the scroll the dates she was born and died, and marked them. We then found several pictures of her and glued them below her dates. The children could see what she looked like and the kind of clothing worn during that period.

Each time we read the biographies of explorers, authors, presidents, or church leaders, we did the same thing. Pretty soon we all had a grasp of who lived when and what events took place during their lifetimes.

History has become my favorite subject! Even more significant, I learned that God's wisdom is available to all who ask for it—in every area of their lives.

Today's Prayer
Dear Lord, thank you for the wisdom you give when we simply ask for it.

Just for Today
Make your own history scroll and watch history come alive.

FORTY-FIVE

A Troubled Heart

Like one who takes off a garment on a cold day, or like vinegar on soda, is he who sings songs to a troubled heart.

PROVERBS 25:20

As I sipped a cup of coffee with a dear friend, we chatted about our families, her business, school, and a myriad of other topics. At one point I began to describe the new method of teaching history that I was trying out. I was excited about making and using our time line scroll. I was shocked when in the middle of a sentence Carol put her head in her hands and began to cry. It took awhile for me to comfort her and finally understand the reason for her tears.

Carol had homeschooled all of her children for a couple of years, but the demands of her business had directed her to put all but her Katie back in public school. Katie, an impressionable six, would go to her mother's restaurant and keep herself busy while her mom was working. During slow times they were able to get into the reading books Carol had bought. Yet Katie's education extended far beyond learning letters. She greeted customers, handed out menus, brought change, and did a host of other things that teenagers can have trouble with.

One particularly busy month, Katie's books had gone untouched. Then one of her customers made a comment about Katie's getting behind, and Carol had had a troubled heart ever since. She was feeling like a failure for what she hadn't been able to do with Katie, and here I was going on and on about all the great things we were getting done. We talked for awhile, prayed together, and came up with a plan that would help

Carol get in teaching time with Katie in the afternoon and evening.

We have all been in Carol's shoes. There are days when we feel as though we are the worst teachers possible for our children. Then along comes a friend having a great school year and it's like salt on an open wound. This experience with Carol helped me to be more sensitive to other homeschooling parents who might be having an off day, week, or month.

Today's Prayer

Dear Heavenly Father, help us to see beyond the words and into the troubled heart. Give us the sensitivity for others that we would want them to have for us on our "down" days.

Just for Today

Call another homeschooling mom today and ask her how you can pray for her.

FORTY-SIX

A Perfect Child

And we urge you, brethren, admonish the unruly, encourage the faithhearted, help the weak, be patient with all men.

1 THESSALONIANS 5:14

Do you feel pressure to have "perfect" children? Do you feel like the whole world is waiting to jump on you when they mess up?

Our children are going to sin. They are going to fight with their siblings, they are going to make inappropriate comments to adults, and they are going to burp and then laugh about it. They are going to be human.

They are also going to complain about school like any normal child. When a public or private school child complains about having to get up early, complains about his or her teachers, or dreams about playing baseball rather than doing math, do we panic? Of course not! But when our homeschooled children have those same complaints, we panic because someone might think our educational system is abusing or inhibiting them. If your children don't wish they were swimming or skiing instead of diagramming sentences, I would say they are more than unique!

Years ago I was using a curriculum that put a lot of pressure on the outward behavior of our children. I found myself apologizing to other parents day and night for the least little infraction my children would have in front of them. I was a basket case, my children were close to needing Valium, and our friends and family were feeling very uncomfortable around us. Finally one wise (and brave) friend put his arms around my husband and me one day and said, "News flash: you're not perfect! Second news flash: God doesn't expect you to be. Final news flash: your friends don't expect you to be, either. So relax!"

It's still a balancing act, but it's getting better. Once we are caught up in the perfectionism trap, it takes time to "deprogram" that way of thinking and to learn how to live in the freedom of real holiness. We will always have people around us who do not have kind things to say about our children and choices, but we have to remember that we work for the Lord, and pleasing him is what counts most.

So relax!

Today's Prayer

Dear Heavenly Father, sometimes all we can see are the negative things in our children, and we fear that they reflect poorly on us. Help us to see our children as you see them and not to put pressure on them or ourselves to be "perfect."

Just for Today

Help your children see how imperfect you were as a child by telling them about a time when you really messed up.

FORTY-SEVEN

The Perfect Father

*And I shall give them one heart, and shall put a new spirit with-
in them. And I shall take the heart of stone out of their flesh and
give them a heart of flesh, that they may walk in My statutes and
keep My ordinances, and do them. Then they will be My people,
and I shall be their God.*

EZEKIEL 11:19-20

Catherine came up to me at a homeschooling conference
and asked if she could speak with me privately. She, her
husband, and their four children had come to our National
Homeschool Family Retreat the year before, and she wanted
me to know what a difference it had made in her husband's life.

According to Catherine, her husband had come home from
the conference determined to become a dedicated, thoughtful
homeschool dad. In the process, it seemed as though he discovered his children all over again.

Just ten days ago her husband had been killed instantly in a
car wreck. She was still in the process of sorting everything out,
but one thing she did know. She was going to continue to
homeschool. "He was passionate about our homeschooling
after the conference," she said, "and I know this is what he
would want me to continue to do."

I think of Catherine when I hear homeschooling moms
complain about their husbands. In our early years of homeschooling I was very critical of Terry. I expected him to be the
perfect father, and I compared him to other homeschooling
dads I met. Then in 1986 Terry had a heart attack and ended
up in ICU for ten days, and I came face-to-face with the reality

that I could lose him. The Lord used that situation to show me what a great husband and father he was and how I had taken him for granted.

I meet all kinds of homeschooling dads. Some take on part of the teaching; others work more than one job so that their wives can stay home and teach. Still others are great with field trips. I also meet many single moms who are handling the load by themselves. No matter what the family dynamics are, we must remember that the perfect Father is the one in heaven, not on earth.

Today's Prayer
O God, thank you for the gift of a truly great husband.

Just for Today
Pray for single parents who are homeschooling their children.

FORTY-EIGHT
Liberty

Now the Lord is the Spirit; and where the Spirit of the Lord is, there is liberty.

2 CORINTHIANS 3:17

I go through phases when it comes to cooking. My "fast food" phase is one that my children particularly love. Frozen entrees, drive-through dinners, and prepackaged meals are standard fare when we have meetings, conferences, or deadlines.

My "exotic phase" hits when I feel that we are in a rut. I'll dig out recipe books with gourmet dishes and spend hours creating masterpieces.

My "healthy phase" always comes after we've battled colds or the flu. This is my children's least favorite phase. When salads, legumes, and tofu hit the plates, my children's eyes roll to the back of their heads!

"Where the Spirit of the Lord is, there is liberty!" I love having the liberty of adjusting meals to fit my family's lifestyle.

The same liberty applies to our homeschooling. Although there are some legal requirements for homeschooling in some states, there are no laws dictating what books you have to use, what supplies are necessary, or during which hours in the day learning must take place. All these things will change as our lifestyles change. The schedule we kept when I was pregnant changed after the baby came. The books and materials I used when I had only one child in school changed when I had seven.

We have the liberty to make adjustments all the time. We can get so comfortable in our surroundings and our current system that we hesitate to make adjustments when they are needed.

Families using prepackaged, one-size-fits-all homeschooling materials will often experience frustration in this area. But just as we have the liberty to make pizza or chicken for dinner, we have the liberty to select and use the teaching materials and methods our families need.

Today's Prayer

Heavenly Father, thank you for the liberty you give us in every area of our lives. Help us to use that liberty wisely. Help us not to be afraid to make changes when we need to.

Just for Today

Break from whatever cooking phase you are in right now and come up with something totally different for dinner one night this week. Make peanut butter pizza, eat by candlelight only, or let the children start with dessert first.

FORTY-NINE

The Exodus

And when Israel saw the great power which the Lord had used against the Egyptians, the people feared the Lord, and they believed in the Lord and in His servant Moses.

EXODUS 14:31

Even after watching the Egyptians suffer through the ten plagues and after being spared themselves, there were some Israelites who had doubts about following Moses. It wasn't until the Red Sea was parted that "the people feared the Lord, and they believed in the Lord and in His servant Moses" (Ex 14:31).

Some of the Israelites trusted in what God was doing even before the first plague came. Still others lost faith at the first sign of trouble, even after seeing with their own eyes all that God had done on their behalf.

I have seen the same responses among homeschoolers. There are families who began homeschooling before they technically knew what to call it. They trusted and feared God, not knowing how the test scores would come out and not knowing whether their children would eventually be accepted into colleges or universities.

Other families explored what materials were available before they got on board. Still others waited until homeschooling families were receiving scholarships and appointments to the Air Force Academy before they took the plunge. And finally there are families who, after seeing all the success in homeschooling and recognizing it as a calling from God, bail out at the first sign of difficulty.

Homeschooling is not just about education; it is about obedience. God is the one who blesses us with children and tells us what educational system to use with them. If he leads us to homeschool our children, he will provide everything we need to accomplish the task.

Just as there were times when the children of Israel waited for water to flow from a rock and picked up manna and quail from the ground, God's provision for our children will seem unconventional as compared to what the world knows and understands. But the honor and glory God receives from this simple step of obedience will make every step of the trip worthwhile.

Today's Prayer

Heavenly Father, just like the children of Israel, sometimes we are tempted to doubt our ability to homeschool. Thank you for the testimonies and encouragement of those who have gone before us and for your miraculous provision.

Just for Today

Ask the children beforehand how many of the plagues they can remember. Then turn to Exodus 7 and read the account.

FIFTY

The Standard

There shall be one standard for you; it shall be for the stranger as well as the native, for I am the Lord your God.

LEVITICUS 24:22

There are times when it doesn't pay to try to be all things to all people. For years I tried to accommodate the many different preferences and convictions of the homeschooling families with whom I came into contact.

Christmas was an especially difficult time of the year. I made notes as to which families didn't approve of Santa Claus or Christmas trees, and placed our holiday decorations in a room that could be avoided during an evening of entertainment.

However, offering hospitality to certain families presented special challenges throughout the year. Some families followed dietary laws found in Leviticus, so when they came to dinner it always included homemade bread, no pork, and lots of grains. Other families were vegetarians, so pot roasts were out. After dinner, some families wanted their children and mine within earshot and eyeshot at all times. Others wanted all the kids outside so that they could talk.

I wanted to serve my guests and make them feel comfortable, but in doing so I found myself going so far as to hide the Twinkies so my "health-food friends" wouldn't be offended! I also felt that I wound up sending mixed messages to my children by trying to live up to my guests' expectations even when I didn't necessarily share their convictions. It wasn't so bad that we ate tofu one day and burgers the next, but I didn't want my children to get caught up in a web of hypocrisy and legalism.

In the end we decided enough was enough, and began to establish our own family standard—what we desired, preferred, and were convicted by God to do. Soon we discovered that this standard was well received by any visitor in our home. We also learned that this same principle applies to homeschooling.

There are a wide variety of homeschooling philosophies, and many "experts" have strong convictions about certain aspects of homeschooling: textbooks, schedules, methods, and plans. It was easy to get caught up in the latest homeschooling method or philosophy. Yet by setting up a family "homeschool standard" we were able to integrate ideas that fit into the overall structure without causing a lot of confusion and disruption to our system.

Our primary goal as parents is to please the Lord, and to trust him and obey his direction for our lives. As long as we maintain that focus—rather than trying to please everyone else—peace and liberty will prevail.

Today's Prayer

Heavenly Father, thank you for the standards you give to us in your Word and for the many ways available to meet those standards.

Just for Today

Have your children write down their favorite color and dessert on a piece of paper. See how well you know one another by guessing what they are.

FIFTY-ONE

A Blessing

You are altogether beautiful, my darling, and there is no blemish in you.

SONG OF SOLOMON 4:7

From the day of his birth, my son Ben was fiercely independent. He was so daring, rugged, and completely unafraid, we got in the habit of calling him a "tough nut" when he was about eighteen months old.

By the time he was three, Ben was already living up to his nickname. He didn't play well with other children, bullied his older brother, and wasn't very kind to our pets. While attending a parenting conference, we were told that children will become what we encourage them to be. We learned that if we praise children for being tidy or kind, they will strive to be even kinder and tidier, just to receive more praise and live up to our expectations. On the other hand, if we continually tell children that they are mean or stupid, they will live up to those expectations as well.

We were convicted about our tough-nut assessment of Ben, and began to praise him for any signs of gentleness we saw in him. When he walked by the cat and petted him instead of kicking him out of the way, we praised him. When he showed any signs of gentleness, no matter how small, we called him "Gentle Ben." Within a few short weeks we noticed a major change in him. He was becoming a very gentle boy! Not a sissy—gentle!

Today Ben is still the one who will do flips and somersaults off the railing. He even took first place in "mutton bustin'" at the National Western Stock Show one year. (For you city folk, mutton bustin' is where you ride a sheep bareback!) Yet in all of his daring exploits, he is still our Gentle Ben, with a tender heart toward God and others.

The power to bless and curse is held in our tongues. Blessing our children and praising them for who they are and the good things they do is the best part of any education we can give them.

Today's Prayer

Heavenly Father, help us find the good in our children today. Keep us from criticizing them unnecessarily.

Just for Today

Write a love note to each of your children, praising them for godly character that you see in them and for how well they are doing in school.

FIFTY-TWO

To Give Honor

The Lord bless you, and keep you; the Lord make His face shine on you, and be gracious to you; the Lord lift up His countenance on you, and give you peace.

NUMBERS 6:24-26

While my mother-in-law lay dying in our home, we had only a short time to say all that we wanted to say. After she was gone we thought of many things we loved about her but never told her, and it weighed heavy on our hearts. With that experience in the back of our minds, we purposed not to let opportunities like that slip through our fingers in the future.

That is when the Lord gave us the idea of Honor Night. Once a week we select a member of the family to honor. A special candle or lantern is placed before the person, which he or she gets to light. During dinner each person has an opportunity to honor that family member. We share how much that person means to us, and give specific examples of how he or she has blessed our lives. Each member, from the youngest to the oldest, learns how to honor others and participates in the joy.

Eventually we extended this tradition to include guests we had for dinner, and we have witnessed grown men and women cry as we honor them at our table. So many people go through life not ever knowing how they have blessed the lives of others. "Honor Nights" help our children look for the good in others, even in their brothers and sisters. They also encourage us to keep on trying to make a difference in someone else's life.

One night when I was the recipient of the honor ritual, I was surprised when one of my children praised me because I had given her a neck and back rub while she sat next to me reading a story in school. I had had no idea that the simple gesture meant so much to her, and I've continued to do it ever since.

Words of affirmation are among the best educational tools available—and the best part about them is that they're free. Honoring one another teaches communication skills that our children will need throughout their lives.

Today's Prayer

Heavenly Father, thank you for the words of blessing and encouragement you are always sending our way through our families and others. Help us affirm our families and others on a regular basis.

Just for Today

Light a candle at dinner and honor everyone at the table by telling them about a very special characteristic you see in them.

FIFTY-THREE

A High Price

However, the king said to Araunah, "No, but I will surely buy it from you for a price, for I will not offer burnt offerings to the Lord my God which cost me nothing." So David bought the threshing floor and the oxen for fifty shekels of silver.

2 SAMUEL 24:24

In 2 Samuel 24, the prophet Gad directed David to erect an altar to the Lord on the threshing floor of Araunah the Jebusite, and to offer a burnt offering because of the sin he had committed by taking a census. David offered to buy the land for the altar, and Araunah graciously offered to give it to him. But David refused. He would not offer a burnt offering to the Lord that had cost him nothing. Instead he bought the floor and offered the sacrifice, which moved the Lord to hold back a plague from Israel.

Rita, a homeschooling mom, was sitting at her kitchen table with an inquiring family, giving information about homeschooling. They were gathering as much data as they could before making their decision. They were concerned about the cost, afraid they would have to pay fees to the state in order to homeschool their children. Rita assured them that homeschooling wouldn't cost them anything other than their books and materials.

Later on that evening, Rita's fourteen-year-old son came to her and said, "Mom, you weren't honest with that family today."

"What do you mean?"

"Well, you told them homeschooling wouldn't cost them

anything. It's cost you your life. You've given up doing a lot of things so that you can teach us and provide us with a good education. Thanks, Mom."

Rita noticed a significant change in her son from that day on. He had calculated the cost and realized he was being given one of the most expensive educations a boy could have.

Some days I wonder if my children realize how much it is costing me to educate them. There are days when I feel taken for granted and wish they were more appreciative of my efforts. But there is joy and satisfaction in knowing that the Lord will use my sacrifice in a mighty way.

Today's Prayer
Heavenly Father, thank you for the opportunity to sacrifice some of our wants, desires, and goals for our families. Take our sacrifice and use it for your honor and glory.

Just for Today
Thank God for the ultimate sacrifice of his Son. No sacrifice we make can ever compare to that.

FIFTY-FOUR
Comparisons

For we are not bold to class or compare ourselves with some of those who commend themselves; but when they measure themselves by themselves, and compare themselves with themselves, they are without understanding.

2 CORINTHIANS 10:12

Mr. and Mrs. Strong have their master's degrees, he in business and she in education, so we found it strange when they came to us wanting help to homeschool. Together we selected a curriculum, set up their program, and became very good friends.

Carrie Strong was also an accomplished musician who played the violin, piano, and a number of other instruments. Whenever I would visit her I would see a flurry of activity and excited students working on projects.

It wasn't long before a visit with Carrie triggered a day or two of depression. As I compared my teaching to hers, my children to hers, and my house to hers, mine always came up short. Soon doubts about my own homeschooling began to surface. Was I really doing what was best for my children? How could I give them the musical instruction they needed? Would they be better off in a public school?

I began to avoid the Strong house. After I hadn't been by for several weeks, Carrie called to invite my children and me over for a day. I kept making excuses about the day and time until she finally said, "Vicki, please, I need you."

As the children played, Carrie sipped on tea and poured out her heart to me. To my amazement, she began comparing her children to mine. "Your children are so social, so confident, and so full of life and fun," she went on. "Mine seem so inhibited and fearful around strangers." On the one hand she missed our visits, she said, but on the other hand she felt depressed for days afterward. I burst out laughing! Then I told her about my own fears, and we laughed together.

We get into a lot of trouble when we begin to compare ourselves. I do watch what other mothers are doing and have gotten some great ideas as a result. I've also seen some things that other families are doing and can say that it would never work in my family. That's OK. Watch for new ideas, and trust the Lord to give you wisdom about what will work best for your family.

Today's Prayer
Heavenly Father, thank you for the uniqueness of our families. Thank you for the skills and abilities you have given to all of us.

Just for Today
At dinner, give out a special certificate to each member of the family that reflects a quality unique to them. For instance, one could be given the "Diligence Award," another a certificate for kindness or self-control.

FIFTY-FIVE

Trade-Offs

*But examine everything carefully; hold fast to that which is good;
abstain from every form of evil.*

1 THESSALONIANS 5:21-22

Today many parents who are contemplating whether to homeschool their children consider homeschooling from a weights-and-scales perspective. They compare the pros and cons of homeschooling against those of sending their children to a public or private school. What will they have to give up to homeschool? What will they gain?

I encourage these families to examine the trade-offs. For instance, if you choose to homeschool, your children can pretty much kiss the senior prom good-bye. They will not have a class ring, tryouts for cheerleading, or hall passes. Are these things you feel your children can live without?

On the other hand, if you choose homeschooling, your children will enjoy another set of benefits: individualized curriculum, a four-hour-a-day school schedule, time with their family, and a teacher who cares about them more than anyone else in the world.

If your children are struggling with all the things they think they are missing by not going to public school, have them make two lists: one for all the benefits and negatives of homeschooling and one for all the benefits and negatives of public or private school. In some cases you'll discover that—with a little creativity, tenacity, and research—your child may not have to miss out on the positive aspects of a public or private school. Homeschool choirs, bands, orchestras, sports teams, and competitions have all been created by homeschooling families who decided they weren't willing to let their children go without these functions.

But in all your thinking and planning about your children's education, examine each aspect for its godly qualities. Some parts of education may be common and traditional, but are they godly? Will a certain tradition help your child to "hold fast to that which is good; abstain from every form of evil"? One of the greatest benefits of homeschooling is being able to address your children's long-term spiritual needs. This is vital, even if that means having to pass up a few traditions along the way.

Today's Prayer

Heavenly Father, we know that we are products of our past educational experiences. Help us sift through what is good, better, and best for our children and examine very carefully the trade-offs.

Just for Today

Talk to your children about the trade-offs they get when they become Christians—such as trading hell for heaven.

FIFTY-SIX

Cause and Effect

Do not be deceived, God is not mocked; for whatever a man sows, this he will also reap. For the one who sows to his own flesh shall from the flesh reap corruption, but the one who sows to the Spirit shall from the Spirit reap eternal life.

GALATIANS 6:7-8

One year my son James was given a toy rifle for his birthday. It was the coveted toy around the house for weeks. While playing with a group of children downtown at a community gathering, a young boy asked James if he could play with his gun. James remembered a discussion we had had in school about sowing seeds of kindness and earning rewards in heaven, so he agreed to let the boy use his gun for an hour.

When the time was up, James returned to the place they had agreed to rendezvous, but the young boy never showed up. He had gone home with James' gun, never to be heard from again.

Later that day when James told me what had happened, I became upset and began to figure out how we could track the boy down. James stopped me and said, "Mom, don't worry about it. I figure I traded the gun for a crown. And I'd rather keep the crown."

From a very young age, children are taught that decisions they make have rewards and consequences. If they touch a hot stove, their fingers will hurt very badly for quite awhile. If they put away their shoes, they will be able to find them again when they need them. If they pull the cat's tail, they will discover the cat has claws and sharp teeth.

The same principles hold true spiritually. An important part of our children's education involves teaching them about this "cause and effect factor." Living in an imperfect world, we can expect that sometimes bad things will happen to good people, and good deeds will sometimes be met with ridicule. Still, we must remind our children that the ultimate cause and effect will be measured in heaven, where all the things done in Jesus' name will bring forth crowns of righteousness.

Today's Prayer

Heavenly Father, sometimes the things we teach our children come full circle. Thank you for our children, and for the lessons we learn from them each day.

Just for Today

Buy a package of flower seeds. Plant a seed with your children every time they sow from the Spirit. Watch the garden grow.

FIFTY-SEVEN

I Have No Friends!

A man of many friends comes to ruin, but there is a friend who sticks closer than a brother.

PROVERBS 18:24

While contemplating a move that would take us out of town and into the mountains, my daughter said, "We can't move there. I'll have no friends!"

"You'll make new friends," I said, but my words seemed to fall on deaf ears. One day after we had moved I heard her brother ask her to play a game of Monopoly. I stopped working in the kitchen long enough to observe the look on her face.

At first she looked puzzled. This was the kid who had tracked dirt on every kitchen floor she had ever cleaned. She was eight years old when he was born, so she still remembered changing his diapers. And now he wanted to play a game of Monopoly with her!

To my surprise, I heard her say, "OK."

They played, he hung in there for the whole game, and she won. All in all, they had a great time. Two days later she received some birthday money in the mail and asked if she could invite one of her friends over for the day and go to lunch at one of the local restaurants. She called every friend in the book but no one was available.

"See, Mom, I have no friends, living this far away from everyone. I have money to go to lunch and do some shopping in town and no one to enjoy it with. I have no friends."

"You could go with your girlfriends another time, when one of them is available."

"I really wanted to use it to celebrate my birthday this weekend.... It won't be much of a birthday celebration if it's next *month!*"

"What about your brother?"

She admitted she had never looked at her brother as a "friend" and wasn't even sure how to do it. But rather than stay home that weekend, she reluctantly decided to invite her brother to go along with her.

While they were in town, my children made a wonderful discovery: They were friends. This revelation surprised them, because they had never really tried to get to know each other. Once they stopped looking for friends outside the family, however, they recognized a wonderful kinship right under their noses!

Since then my kids have continued to develop that friendship. Sometimes they will go to lunch, depending upon who has money. Other times they'll just play a game together. But since that day, I have not heard either of them say, "I have no friends!"

Today's Prayer

Dear Lord, help our children learn to cultivate deep friendships right in their own families; friendships that will last a lifetime.

Just for Today

If you have two children that seem to struggle with each other, give them a couple of bucks and let them have a date at the local ice cream parlor.

FIFTY-EIGHT
En Garde!

Do not love the world, nor the things in the world.... For all that is in the world, the lust of the flesh and the lust of the eyes and the boastful pride of life, is not from the Father, but is from the world.
1 JOHN 2:15-16

I love swashbuckling movies! One of my favorites is *The Three Musketeers*, with Gene Kelly. While watching these movies I've noticed that before any swordplay, someone warns, *"En garde!"* which, loosely translated, means "Watch out!"

Today's verse is like an *"en garde"* from the Lord. He gives us three positions from which the enemy will attack us: the lust of the flesh, the lust of the eyes, and the boastful pride of life. In school as we read biographies and follow current events in the newspapers, I ask my children to watch for the area of attack in a person's life. The lust of the flesh results in immorality—affairs or unnatural relationships. The lust of the eyes reveals itself in greed. The boastful pride of life usually translates to power or control, and is seen in the person who tries to crush those who get in his or her way.

When we look at historical figures such as politicians, kings, military leaders, scientists, and even preachers, if they have fallen it is always because of greed, immorality, power, or a combination of all three.

We have worked out a code within our family. When we see someone in a position where immorality, greed, or power is a threat, we simply say, *"En garde."* That simple phrase helps them get a reality check when they are lingering too long on a lingerie ad in the newspaper, fighting over a toy, pushing a brother or sister around, choosing questionable videos in the rental store, and so on. As long as there is breath in our bodies, we all need to be *"en garde."*

Today's Prayer

Dear Lord, the pressure to love the world is so great. Help our children to resist and flee youthful lusts. Help us as parents to recognize the attacks when they come and to stand in the battle with our children.

Just for Today

Let your children make swords out of cardboard. Shine a light so that it casts a shadow behind them, and let them fence their shadow as they pretend they are fighting the "things of the world."

FIFTY-NINE

Pioneers and Settlers

Unless the Lord builds the house, they labor in vain who build it; unless the Lord guards the city, the watchman keeps awake in vain.

PSALM 127:1

Any homeschool veteran will tell you that the "good old days" in homeschooling weren't so good! In many places parents homeschooled in secret, knowing they risked imprisonment and that their children could be taken from them if the wrong people discovered what they were doing.

These families often lived somewhat reclusive lives, and could be considered a bit "odd" even by families who began homeschooling more recently.

On the other hand, these "old-timers" shake their heads when they see new homeschoolers take their freedom to homeschool lightly. "The new crop of homeschoolers," they say, "will never hold up under the pressure if the powers that be try to stamp out homeschooling!"

I think both groups have a point, but a better point to be made is found in today's verse and the history of our country.

As our country was forming and the border pushing farther and farther west, we had two groups of people, the pioneers and the settlers. The pioneers were brave, and thrived on new challenges. They dared to go where no man had gone before. If it weren't for the pioneers, our country would be confined to the eastern shores.

Once the new land was explored, in came the settlers. These were the folks who had the patience to clear the land, plant crops, and stabilize the wilderness. If it weren't for the settlers, we wouldn't have farms, towns, and cities.

Both groups were determined and set in their ways. Just as trouble came when the settlers wouldn't heed the advice of the pioneers, progress was stifled when the pioneers wouldn't accept the settlers' right to come behind.

God has used both pioneers and settlers to build the homeschooling movement in this country, and it is important that we understand and appreciate one another. The bridges we build with one another today could determine the progress of homeschooling in the future.

Today's Prayer

Dear Lord, thank you for establishing homeschooling as a viable educational choice in this country and for watching over our freedom to choose it.

Just for Today

Begin reading *Little House in the Big Woods* by Laura Ingalls Wilder with your children.

SIXTY

A Good Name

A good name is to be more desired than great riches, favor is better than silver and gold.

PROVERBS 22:1

Everyone was excited when a puppy came to join the Brady home. He was a darling collie that came with everything he needed except a name.

Everyone offered suggestions, but since there was no consensus we decided to draw names from a hat. Before the children put their suggestions on a piece of paper, we discussed what kind of name would be appropriate. This led us to the question of what makes a name good or bad.

A great discussion followed. It was agreed that all names start out very good or at least neutral, but that some end up being bad because of how a specific person lived when he or she had that name. Names like Judas, Delilah, Jezebel, and Lucifer were unthinkable as names for this pet because of the reputations of their previous owners. Samson was considered a good name because he was able to redeem his reputation before he died.

As we discussed names we talked to the children about their own names. They each started out life with a name that had been worn by saints before them with great honor and distinction. When we read or hear of people who share our name, we naturally want to know all about them. What did they accomplish in their lives, and were their actions good or bad? Did they have hearts for God?

We reminded the children that once they accepted Jesus

Christ as their personal Savior, they had a new name to live up to: Christian. This name is the one that will be the most difficult to live up to. Will others want to be a Christian after knowing us and seeing the testimony of our lives?

After the discussion was over we agreed on a name for our new pet—the Angel Gabriel, or "Gabe" for short. Gabe was named partly for the crop of snowy white hair on his neck ... and partly for his job in our home. Living in the mountains with bears and mountain lions, we needed a dog that would alert us to danger and protect the children from harm. So far, he barks at all the deer that come into the yard and watches over our pet rabbit. He's living up to his name!

Today's Prayer
Dear Father in heaven, thank you for adopting us and giving us your name. Help us never to dishonor it.

Just for Today
On one set of index cards, write the names of the members of your family. On a second set of index cards, write the meaning of each name. Put all the cards on the table and see how many your children can match up.

Just Because

For God so loved the world, that He gave His only begotten Son, that whoever believes in Him should not perish, but have eternal life.

JOHN 3:16

Each of my children has assigned chores, from the youngest to the oldest. Some of the chores have to be done daily, such as feeding the rabbit and getting the newspaper. Others, like dusting and cleaning out the vehicles, are done once a week.

Some weeks getting chores done can be a real battle. The verbal assaults and vacuum tug-of-wars can be irritating, and at times I've been known to "blow up." One week was particularly bad: the same battles erupted over and over, and my temper flared up. I cooled off quickly, however, when I overheard my five-year-old admonish her three-year-old sister.

"You'd better get your work done," she said as she shook her pointed finger, "or don't expect Mommy to love you."

I was horrified! I sat down on the steps and tried to fathom what I had just heard. Was that really what they believed? Did they really think that my love for them was based on their ability to perform their chores? As I thought back through the week I could see how they had gotten that impression. The only time I had praised them verbally or given hugs and kisses was when they had done their work.

Gathering my children together, I apologized to them for my temper that week. More than anything I wanted them to understand that I love them "just because," not for anything they do to deserve it.

Our love for our children must never be based on how well they do their schoolwork, how many gifts they give us, or how quickly and efficiently they get their chores done. Our love is especially needed when they mess up or fail. Maybe that's why my children find John 3:16 so appealing: *For God so loved the world* ... just because.

Today's Prayer

Heavenly Father, thank you for loving us just because. Help us communicate an unconditional love for our children.

Just for Today

Memorize John 3:16 if you haven't already. Recite it often throughout the day.

SIXTY-TWO

In the End

I have fought the good fight, I have finished the course, I have kept the faith.

2 TIMOTHY 4:7

One of my all-time favorite movies is *The Big Country*, starring Gregory Peck. In the movie Peck's character is an Easterner visiting his fiancée in the Wild West. Throughout the story this man is misunderstood and perceived to be a coward. When he does not take measures to disprove his cowardice, even his fiancée doubts him.

The most important moment in the whole movie is when he turns to his fiancée and says, "I'm not responsible for what people think, only for what I am!"

There are going to be times when we are misunderstood for the homeschooling decisions we make. People thought we were cultists when we first began homeschooling. Through the years other homeschoolers have been labeled right-wing fanatics, child abusers, religious zealots, and educational idiots. These attacks have come from teachers, school administrators, the media, pastors, employers, neighbors, and even grandparents.

It takes a great deal of personal fortitude to stand up under such attacks. It can be tempting to react and sling the same slurs in the opposite direction. Some homeschoolers decide to withdraw from all public life, provoking an "I told you so!" from their critics. Others redouble their efforts in an attempt to graduate their children early and prove their critics wrong.

I've had the labels. I still get the labels. I've had visitors sidle up to my children, put a book in their hands, and ask them to read, just to make sure they can. I've had relatives and neighbors criticize my daughter's spelling, forgetting that the doctors had predicted she would never be able to read or write at all.

At the end of the movie, Gregory Peck was vindicated. Real life isn't always like that. Vindication may not ever come in this life—and it certainly won't come by pressuring our children to do well. Yet Peck's declaration *is* true to life: we're not responsible for what other people think, only for what we are.

If we are obedient to the Lord as he calls us to homeschool, then in the end, that's all the vindication we will need.

Today's Prayer

Dear Father, help us to ignore the criticisms of others and to teach our children in a way that will please and honor you.

Just for Today

Take a break from school, rent *The Big Country,* pop up a batch of popcorn, and enjoy.

SIXTY-THREE

Tired of Being Good

But as for you, brethren, do not grow weary of doing good.
2 THESSALONIANS 3:13

I wish I could bottle whatever it is that makes our kids wake up happy and good as gold in the morning. It doesn't happen every day, but when it does the whole day is golden.

Recently my five-year-old, Connie, woke up full of sunshine—singing, giving hugs and kisses to everyone, and wearing a bright smile from one corner of her face to the other. All morning she was a jewel.

Three-year-old Anna didn't seem to care for the extra praise her big sister was getting all morning. Anna seemed determined to "bring her down." Just after lunch, despite all of our warnings, Anna teased one time too many and Connie let her have it.

After the fray I sat down with Connie and asked her why she hit her sister. Connie sighed a big sigh and said, "Well Mom, I guess I just ran out of 'good.'"

There are days when I, too, feel I have just "run out of good." These days come when the children don't seem to care about their education and I have to beg, plead, and threaten them to get their schoolwork done. It happens when I find myself bandaging feelings all day because the children have been fussing at each other. It happens again when a friend calls and asks me to go to lunch with "the girls" and I can't because I have a million school projects already planned.

On days like these I find I need to go to my room, get out my Bible, and recall all the "good" Jesus has done for me. He never "runs out of good." If we keep open our lines of communication with him, we will have an endless source of "good." Jesus knows what we sometimes forget: the good we are doing on earth now will count for all eternity.

Today's Prayer

Dear Lord, thank you for never "running out of good" on our behalf. Help us keep that in mind today as we raise our children.

Just for Today

Read Genesis 1 out loud to your children and have them count how many times the word *good* is used.

SIXTY-FOUR

Heavenly Minded

If then you have been raised up with Christ, keep seeking the things above, where Christ is, seated at the right hand of God. Set your mind on the things above, not on the things that are on earth.

COLOSSIANS 3:1-2

As part of a history lesson we listened to a tape-recorded testimony of a missionary who had been taken prisoner during World War II. She lost her husband, endured imprisonment, and suffered physically and emotionally during those years. She survived because of her personal relationship with Jesus Christ and her knowledge of his Word. Recalling Scripture verses she had learned through the years brought her comfort, encouragement, and peace.

Y2K predictions, biological warfare, earthquakes, volcanoes, asteroids, and other potential disasters have been portrayed recently on the news, in books, and in movies. I've often wondered what we would do as a family if calamity struck.

As I listened to the biography, I was reminded that the most important thing my children will ever know is God's Word. Math, science, reading, writing, history, and such are important parts of our children's education, especially for those preparing to take college entrance exams. Yet, the truths of Scripture are just as vital when it comes to meeting the challenges of life.

Think of the challenges your children will face. What will sustain them as they face college exams? How will they work through difficult relationships? Where will they turn when they must learn how to work for a non-Christian boss, or choose a spouse? The Word of God is an unfailing source of wisdom and guidance in all these situations.

Good writing and math skills are important, and your children may need a grasp of basic chemistry to pursue God's future plans for them. At the same time, our children need to know that God and his Word are the highest priority of all.

Today's Prayer

Dear Lord, as parents we know that what we do speaks louder to our children than what we say. Help us to demonstrate what is most important by putting you and your Word first in our lives.

Just for Today

Take a walk with your children and talk about their—and your—greatest hopes, fears, and dreams for the future.

SIXTY-FIVE
Godly Goals

*But Ruth said, "Do not urge me to leave you or turn back from fol-
lowing you; for where you go, I will go, and where you lodge, I will
lodge. Your people shall be my people, and your God, my God. Where
you die, I will die, and there I will be buried. Thus may the Lord
do to me, and worse, if anything but death parts you and me."*

RUTH 1:16-17

Once a year we hear about "Take Your Daughter to Work
Day." Mothers are encouraged to take their daughters
out of school and allow them to spend the day with them on
the job. The purpose of this exercise is to help these impressionable girls aspire to a career outside the home.

As Christian parents, we have a unique opportunity to "take
our children to work" and instill in them a deep appreciation
and respect for the most important career of all: being godly
spouses and parents. By doing this, we can counter the negative messages about the importance of family that our culture
feeds young children.

What should you do if one or more of your children decide
that they want to become "at home" mothers and use that as
an excuse to grumble about algebra, English, or other subjects?
It's important to be sensitive to the leading of the Spirit in our
children's lives, and yet at times a parent's job is to keep our
children "on course." Even if they will only retain the material
long enough to pass the state standardized testing requirements, they will be making good use of God's precious gift to
them: their minds.

Besides, if one or more of our children decide to become

"stay-at-home parents," one should not necessarily rule out college. I look back on my college days and remember how blessed and matured I was by those experiences. College will round out and give an added dimension to anyone's life. And someday they may need this training to educate their own children!

Our daughters need to understand that becoming the best wives, mothers, and homemakers they can possibly be is a wonderful and godly career choice. By the same token, if God calls our sons to a trade school, apprenticeship, or college, we will have given them the skills they need to become godly husbands and fathers as well. As parents, our job is to help our children discern God's calling on their lives, and to guide them to make the best use of their gifts, whatever those might be.

Today's Prayer

Dear Lord, you know the future of our sons and daughters. Guide us as we train them and teach them the things they will need to know to be successful in the future.

Just for Today

If you have a daughter, let her be mom for a day. Reverse your roles and just see how well she does! If you have more than one daughter, let them take turns.

SIXTY-SIX

Marriage 101

Husbands, love your wives, just as Christ also loved the church and gave Himself up for her.

EPHESIANS 5:25

When it comes to training our children about marriage, it's a good idea to begin with our sons. Part of that teaching involves their understanding our role as future mothers-in-law. My husband and I have counseled countless couples, and discovered that well over 90 percent of the problems stem from the mother-and-son relationship.

As mothers, we must train our sons on how they must one day "leave mother and father" and cleave to their wives. Many men today don't know how to do that, and their mothers are often responsible.

As a young girl growing up in an orphanage, I used to dream of the life I would lead as a bride someday. I especially dreamt of our first candlelit Christmas dinner, just my husband and me by the fire. The idea of a potluck at Grandma's never entered my mind.

When I married Terry, I soon discovered that his family got together for all the major holidays, as well as a few of the minor ones: Secretary's Day, Tulip Day, and ... well, you get the picture. I endured my first Thanksgiving with the gang by holding on to my dream of that quiet, romantic, candlelit Christmas.

Although Terry eagerly agreed to my idea, on nearly every day between Thanksgiving and Christmas his mother called and put pressure on us to be with her. Christmas Day came and—you guessed it—we were with his family. For years afterward his mother and I were competitors, and I wasn't ever really sure, if push came to shove, whom my husband would pick.

We eventually sorted out the difficulty, and his mother and I became the best of friends. And yet, these experiences taught me a lesson. I have a responsibility to teach my boys how to "leave and cleave," and to learn what it means to be a good mother-in-law. It's not easy; the old "jealousy factor" can get a foothold if we're not careful.

Training boys in this area can be a lot of fun. Talk to them about hypothetical situations, and encourage them to plan to love their wives just as Christ loved the church and gave himself up for her. At the same time, prepare yourself ahead of time not to have them around for a few Christmas dinners.

Today's Prayer

Dear Lord, thank you for our godly young men. Help us learn how to be the best mothers-in-law we can possibly be.

Just for Today

If you have a son, have a heart-to-heart talk with him and pray with him about his future bride.

SIXTY-SEVEN

What Happens Next?

But we do not want you to be uninformed, brethren, about those who are asleep, that you may not grieve, as do the rest who have no hope.

1 THESSALONIANS 4:13

Last year we got a call from the daughter of one of our eld erly neighbors. She lived an hour away and had tried all day to reach her father on the phone, to no avail. Terry and the three boys raced over to his house and managed to get in and discovered Mr. Hammer lying on the floor. He had fallen and had lain there for hours, unable to get up.

The four of them stayed with him until the ambulance could get him to the hospital. Mr. Hammer was in his eighties, very sick, and not expected to live much longer. I decided the experience had given us a golden opportunity to bring up the subject of death with our children.

The next week in school I gave each of the children a pair of gloves to wear throughout the day. They had to eat, write, count change, and do everything needed in a normal day without taking them off. In the middle of a taco dinner we finally told them to take off the gloves.

We explained to them that the gloves were like the physical body that houses our soul and spirit. Who we really are is inside our bodies, just like their hands in their gloves. When we die, we remove the physical shell, but who we are lives on for eternity.

Just as using the gloves was cumbersome and difficult, being bound to our earthly bodies has its limitations. Death frees us from the earthly trappings and gives us the ability to see, know, and understand God much better. Christians need not fear death, because it reunites us with God, though it separates us temporarily from those we love. However, those who are not Christians *should* fear death, for it will eternally separate them from the Creator in a place called hell.

Mr. Hammer died about two weeks later. We never knew for sure where he stood with the Lord. Although it appeared that he had rejected Jesus while he lived on our mountain, Terry was able to share the Lord with him while he was in the hospital. We hope someday to see him in heaven.

Today's Prayer

Dear Lord, thank you for sending your Son to die for us so that we can spend eternity with you.

Just for Today

Put some gloves on and share the spiritual application with your children.

SIXTY-EIGHT

When the Mockers Come

Know this first of all, that in the last days mockers will come with their mocking, following after their own lusts, and saying, "Where is the promise of His coming? For ever since the fathers fell asleep, all continues just as it was from the beginning of creation."

2 PETER 3:3 4

I love to go camping as a family. There is something about the smell of a smoldering campfire, toasted marshmallows, and a freshly washed forest. One year we went camping with some friends and took our three-year-old nephew with us. He and my then three-year-old Sam were inseparable the whole weekend.

While packing up to head for home the boys came to me and with full mouths said, "Good gwapes!" Good grapes? I just nodded and smiled back, until it dawned on me that we hadn't brought any grapes and that I had not seen any wild fruit trees in the area.

Quickly we grabbed a bottle of syrup of ipecac and started spooning it down their throats. They were oblivious to the seriousness of the situation until the syrup began to work its magic. Eventually they were fine, although we never knew for sure what the grapes were (we suspect only rose hips).

There are even greater dangers facing our children today, especially in the public and private school systems. Drugs, violence, alcohol, immorality, and attacks on Christianity can put their souls in jeopardy, and sometimes their physical well-being, too. For all these reasons, more and more families are deciding to take their children out of school.

In some cases, friends and relatives are supportive of this decision, and those homeschooling families are blessed indeed. Most aren't that fortunate. "You're overreacting and overprotecting your children," the mockers say. "People have been going to public and private schools for years, and most systems aren't that bad."

How bad is "that bad"? When we discovered that our children had eaten something that could have poisoned them, we didn't wait to see the effects of the poisoning before doing something about the potential danger. We emptied their stomachs right away. If you see your children in the path of real spiritual or even physical danger, as a parent you have an obligation to protect them.

Today's Prayer

Dear Lord, help us stand strong when others mock us for homeschooling. Remind us daily of the rewards and benefits it secures for their future.

Just for Today

Check your medicine cabinet and make sure you have a bottle of syrup of ipecac on hand for emergencies.

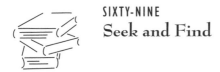

SIXTY-NINE
Seek and Find

Then you will call upon Me and come and pray to Me, and I will listen to you. And you will seek Me and find Me, when you search for Me with all your heart. And I will be found by you.

JEREMIAH 29:12-14a

When my boys were very little we lived on a hobby farm on the outskirts of Denver. One day after lunch I told four-year-old Sam to head down to his bed for a nap. I was in the middle of changing a diaper, but I assured him I would be down to tuck him in shortly.

About ten minutes later I went to find him, but his bed was empty. I called for him, checked the other rooms, and began to fume. I sent Emily outside to check the barn and chicken coop, to no avail. Remembering recent headlines, I began to panic. Two months earlier a mother on a farm only minutes from us had been abducted from her own yard, in front of her children, and murdered.

I ran outside and down the lane, crying and calling for Sam. As far as I could see in both directions, he was nowhere to be found. I went back into the house and called my husband, who raced home. Finally I went to my bedroom and cried out to the Lord, asking him for help. Immediately after my prayer I heard a slight sound from the corner of my room. I walked over to a dirty clothes basket and lifted the lid.

Inside was Sam, fast asleep. Earlier we had been playing hide-and-seek, and now I remembered that it had been his turn to hide when we broke for lunch. I had told him we'd play later but hadn't thought any more about it. He must have continued the game and fallen asleep while waiting to be discovered. Picking him up out of the basket, I wept tears of gratitude that he was safe.

I used to think that finding help from God was much like finding Sam. I pictured God hiding himself and his will from me until I was totally desperate and broken. Nothing could be further from the truth.

There have been times that I have worried and struggled for days over something in school, looking for answers on my own. As soon as I went to the Lord with the problem, peace came, and then the solution. God doesn't play hide-and-seek with us. He is right beside us, ready with every solution to curricula, schedules, finances, and even college. Seek and you really shall find.

Today's Prayer

Dear Lord, thank you for not only calling us to homeschool but also providing everything we need to carry it out.

Just for Today

When's the last time you played hide-and-seek with your children? Why not today?

SEVENTY

It's Not Fair!

Peter therefore seeing him said to Jesus, "Lord, and what about this man?" Jesus said to him, "If I want him to remain until I come, what is that to you? You follow Me!"

JOHN 21:21-22

"**I**t's not fair!"

"What's not?"

"Look at all those kids playing soccer in the field. They don't have to do school today and we do!"

How many times have I heard my children compare themselves with other children? Once again I reminded them of the Tuesday we had canceled school because it was one of their birthdays, yet all the neighborhood kids had been in class.

"And remember the day we took off school and went to help feed the neighbor's dairy cows when Mr. Anderson was sick? As I recall, all the neighborhood children were at their desks. And what about the time ..."

I didn't need to continue. The children reluctantly returned to their work. It wasn't long before the whole discussion was but a blip on their memory banks for the day.

How often do we as adults complain and compare our lives to those of others? One homeschooling family has only two children, so they can afford a full-service curriculum, while another family can afford only a few books and gas to get to and from the library every week.

We see some homeschooling families as being so organized that they can bake bread, take music lessons, and complete their seatwork, all before noon. Other families seem to have children who never complain when asked to change the baby's diaper or vacuum the house.

If you are going to succeed at homeschooling, it's important to ask the Lord to give you a set of "spiritual blinders" so you don't get caught in the comparison trap. If the Lord tells one homeschooling family to participate in sports or choir, "what is that to me?"

When our focus is on the Lord and his will and design for our lives, it is easy to be content and happy in our circumstances. But sideways glances can cause us to become discontent with our own direction or critical of others.

Homeschooling is not a track meet of competing families, it is a calling. And even though the Lord has called thousands to this new educational adventure, no two families have been called alike.

Today's Prayer

Dear Lord, when I am tempted to compare my family and my calling with another's, remind me of your words, "You follow me!"

Just for Today

Place a bowl of fruit or candy in the room, then give each of your children different directions as to how to get to it.

SEVENTY-ONE

Neck to Knees

Now concerning the things about which you wrote, it is good for a man not to touch a woman.

1 CORINTHIANS 7:1

Teaching the academic basics is what most families first think of when they plan to homeschool. But home-schooling allows you to also teach character, discipline, healthy habits, and a whole lot more. One thing essential for our children to learn is modesty and self-protection.

Years ago we came up with a motto in our home:

Neck to knees, nobody sees and … nobody touches.

Even when our children were too young to understand the why behind this little rhyme, they knew that the zone on their bodies between their necks and their knees was private—not to be looked at and not to be touched by anyone else. (When the children asked us about bathing suits, we explained that the rules regarding touch still applied.) Beyond a shadow of a doubt they knew that if anyone violated the privacy rule—brother, sister, relative, or neighbor—they were to let us know immediately.

One day after spending the weekend at a friend's house, my daughter seemed quiet and thoughtful. After prodding her, we discovered that her overnight visit had been a disaster. Her friend's father had urged her to hold his hand in the truck as he brought her to his house, and at the house had repeatedly pulled her to sit on his lap.

His behavior had disturbed my daughter, and at one point she had blurted out, "Neck to knees, nobody sees and nobody touches!" This seemed to curtail his odd behavior for the remainder of her visit. She was too young to understand the reason behind his improper advances, but old enough to sense something was not right.

After an initial cooling-off period, Terry approached the father—a friend and church deacon—and talked to him about his behavior. The man wept and confessed that he had been having a struggle in this area and agreed to get help.

Since that time we have stressed the "neck to knees" principle even more. I shudder to think of what could have happened had we not taught our daughter the rhyme prior to that visit.

Today's Prayer

Heavenly Father, thank you for protecting our children when we can't. Help our children remain pure and undefiled for their future spouses.

Just for Today

Teach your children the phrase "Neck to knees, nobody sees and nobody touches." You may have to make allowances for swimsuit days and diaper changes.

SEVENTY-TWO

The Sparrow

Are not two sparrows sold for a cent? And yet not one of them will fall to the ground apart from your Father. But the very hairs of your head are all numbered. Therefore do not fear; you are of more value than many sparrows.

MATTHEW 10:29-31

Homeschooling is usually a "mom" thing. Although there are fathers that take on the full-time responsibility of teaching their children, in most cases the dads are at work all day and the moms are at home. I never suspected my husband worried about our homeschooling until he told me the following story.

Terry was pastoring a church when one of his deacons made a comment about our homeschooling. Several families had joined the church lately, and all of them homeschooled. The deacon was afraid our church would be perceived as a cult, and suggested that Terry consider putting our children in public school for the sake of his ministry.

Terry carefully began to evaluate his homeschooling decision, recognizing the fact that he could be asked to leave the church over this issue. I was pregnant, we had no savings, and his heart was heavy as he thought about what we would do and where we would go.

One day while Terry was driving down a somewhat deserted highway an unusual thing happened. A huge truck zoomed by, and as it did a small sparrow flew in between the two vehicles. The force of the air slammed the bird into Terry's windshield and bounced it onto the pavement below.

Startled, he pulled over to check the window, which had survived the impact, and the bird, which had not. Just then the Lord reminded him of today's verse. Immediately he was flooded with the peace of God. He knew God had called him to homeschool his children and to pastor the church. Somehow the Lord would work out both.

I have since learned that many fathers worry about the effect homeschooling will have on their children. They are concerned that their children won't get good jobs or that they will be rejected by society. They fret about the pressure the task puts on their wives, and about how that will in turn affect home life. They wonder if it's worth the hassle.

We need to pray for our husbands and encourage them to continue to trust in the Lord for their decision to homeschool. Whether their role is to stay at home and teach or to earn the money the family needs, our husbands' leadership, guidance, and protection is an important part of the homeschooling process.

Today's Prayer

Dear Lord, thank you for the many fathers who work long hours, sacrifice their goals, and shoulder the responsibility for homeschooling their children.

Just for Today

Tell your husband how grateful you are for his leadership and commitment to your family.

SEVENTY-THREE

The Appointed Time

For if you remain silent at this time, relief and deliverance will arise for the Jews from another place and you and your father's house will perish. And who knows whether you have not attained royalty for such a time as this?

ESTHER 4:14

In the third chapter of Esther we read of the wicked Haman. Haman tricked King Xerxes into decreeing that on the thirteenth day of the twelfth month it would be lawful to kill any Jew and take all that belonged to him or her.

The king was not aware that his wife, the beautiful Queen Esther, was herself a Jew. Esther's Uncle Mordecai reminded her that she and all her people could be destroyed if she didn't do something. So, as all the Jews prayed and fasted, Esther courageously took action and saved her people.

For more than thirty years our children have been "caught in the crossfires" of another kind of destructive legislation, making it illegal for our children to be taught about God in our schools. In some cases, children are prevented from even *talking* about him. We now have a generation or more of people who have no clue who Jesus Christ is.

While traveling and living in our motor home, we set up home base in a trailer park in Arizona. There we started a weekly Bible club for the children who lived nearby. To our amazement, we discovered that of the thirty-five children coming to our club, more than half had never heard of Jesus Christ.

Is it possible that God has brought us into homeschooling "for such a time as this"? Homeschooling should not be an end in itself, but a means to an end. It is great that our children know the Lord and are receiving a good education. However, that education and training must not draw us "inward" and keep us isolated from the world around us. We need to share the Lord with others. It won't matter what educational system we use if our family, friends, and neighbors die and go to hell.

There are so many ways we can share the Lord in our communities through our homeschooling. Start a reading club for children in the neighborhood who need extra help. Vacation Bible School, nursing home ministries, and baby-sitting are some other things we can do to reach the lost. What can you do?

Today's Prayer

Dear Lord, the lost are all around us, and sometimes we get so busy with our own families, we forget. Please show us how to use our homeschooling to reach others.

Just for Today

Pray with your family for the unsaved friends, neighbors, and family members in your lives. Ask God for a unique way to use your homeschooling to reach them.

SEVENTY-FOUR

Adolescence

When I was a child, I used to speak as a child, think as a child, reason as a child; when I became a man, I did away with childish things.

1 CORINTHIANS 13:11

As far as I can tell from what I have been told and what I have studied, the word *adolescence* is not in the Bible. When Jewish children turned twelve or thirteen, they were considered men and women. They were given adult responsibilities and earned the respect and privileges that went along with being an adult.

Jesus was twelve years old when he taught in the temple. Most scholars put Mary's age at fourteen when she was pregnant with our Savior.

In today's society our young teens, or "adolescents," have begun their quest for freedom, independence, and responsibility, but in most cases they do not fulfill any meaningful role in society.

The problem is this: Just as children developing fine motor skills as toddlers need to practice with blocks and Legos, our young adults need to exercise and develop their drive for responsibility and independence by assuming new leadership roles within the family, community, and church. Baby-sitting, drilling math facts, filling out lesson plans, setting up field trips, making and taking phone calls, ordering materials, and filling out reports are just a few of the many things we can guide our young adults into doing.

There are also leadership opportunities available outside the home. At different times and ages my children have interned as junior staff aides at the American Red Cross, adopted residents at the local nursing home, and apprenticed as receptionists, clerks, busboys, or dishwashers. As apprentices they were not paid staff, yet some of the businesses were so impressed with their work that they gave them gifts of food, money, and other products.

Although the gifts were nice, the praise and satisfaction of knowing they had successfully accomplished something they had never tried before was reward enough. The maturity they gained outside the home gave them new status and success inside the home.

When this drive for independence comes, we can fight it, ignore it, or look for ways to channel it.

Today's Prayer

Heavenly Father, help me see my children through your eyes and find ways to develop leadership skills in them as they become more independent.

Just for Today

Have a heart-to-heart talk with your children and ask them about ways they would like to serve their community. Make a list and begin to contact businesses and organizations, inquiring about apprenticeships, internships, and ministry opportunities.

SEVENTY-FIVE

A Stranger's Praise

Let another praise you, and not your own mouth; a stranger, and not your own lips.

PROVERBS 27:2

Going out to eat as a family of nine can be quite a production. By the time two tables are pulled together and set, most of the people around are craning their necks to see what's going on.

One Sunday afternoon we went to lunch at a busy restaurant and used the time before the meal arrived to talk about what the children had learned in church that morning. The younger children illustrated their lesson on their place mats with crayons, while the older ones entered into the discussion.

After the food arrived, we said grace together and began to talk about using one of the verses the pastor had given as a memory verse in school for the week. Just about the time we were ready to leave, an elderly couple came up to our table.

"We finished our meal nearly an hour ago," she began, "but we had to stay and watch your family. It has been years since I've seen children with such good deportment and manners. I hope you don't mind, but I eavesdropped into your conversation and I know you homeschool. I was a teacher for over forty years before I retired, and when I first heard about homeschooling ten years ago I thought it was the worst idea of the century. Since then I've come to believe it is the salvation of our nation. God bless you, and keep up the good work."

With that she squeezed my hand, and we watched her through moistened eyes as she went out the door.

We never know who is watching or what they think when it comes to our families. It is not up to us to prove to others that homeschooling can work. It is up to us to be faithful to our calling, and to leave the results and the testimony of what we do up to the Lord.

Today's Prayer
Dear Lord, thank you for the words of encouragement you speak to us through others. It inspires us to do even better.

Just for Today
Take your family out for a meal or for ice cream.

SEVENTY-SIX
Star Gazers

And He took him outside and said, "Now look toward the heavens, and count the stars, if you are able to count them." And He said to him, "So shall your descendants be." Then he believed in the Lord; and He reckoned it to him as righteousness.

GENESIS 15:5-6

Our children's bedrooms have skylights. The kids love to lie down at night and search the sky, gaze at the moon, watch for satellites, and wait for shooting stars.

Studying stars in school, we have found that most books dwell on purely scientific aspects of stars—how far away they are, how they are clustered, and so on. However, just as in every other class, I supplement this information with spiritual truth.

Stars have played a very important role in Scripture. They were created by God in Genesis 1, established forever in Psalm 148, and listed by name in Job 9 and 38. Star worship is forbidden in Deuteronomy 4, and condemned by the prophets in Jeremiah 8. A star was used to lead the wise men and shepherds to the Savior (see Mt 2).

If we teach our children the basic, antiseptic characteristics about our solar system and universe but leave out how it has been greatly used by God, we shortchange their education. Today we have scientists who argue back and forth about the age of the earth and the stars. Countless books have been written about the theories, hypotheses, and proofs for each position. How much time should we spend on examining all sides to this issue? Titus 3:9 says, "But shun foolish controversies and genealogies and strife and disputes about the Law; for they are unprofitable and worthless."

I feel this verse has application to the current controversies in the scientific world about our solar system. The most important thing our children need to know is that God created it and has used his creation to draw men unto himself.

To try to separate the scientific studies of the stars from their spiritual roots and significance is like trying to separate an engine from a car. One isn't productive without the other.

Today's Prayer

Dear Heavenly Father, thank you for the moon and stars that hang in the night. Let their beauty and complications draw men to you.

Just for Today

Take a blanket and lie on the grass with your children tonight. Try to name or even count the stars you see.

SEVENTY-SEVEN

God's Perfect Plan

For as the heavens are higher than the earth, so are My ways higher than your ways, and My thoughts than your thoughts.

ISAIAH 55:9

Politics have always been a passion of mine. I have calluses on my fingers from the calls I have made to elected officials, urging them to vote one way or another on a particular issue.

Too often my efforts have little noticeable impact, a fact that in the beginning left me confused and depressed. Time and again I called on behalf of the unborn, for example, only to discover that the elected official had voted "pro-choice." I watched in horror while bill after bill was introduced to further destroy the definition and sanctity of the family. I couldn't sleep at night, wondering about what else I could do that I hadn't already done. I grieved over the wasted years when I didn't get involved in the political process. The world seemed totally out of control, and I felt powerless to do anything about it.

Then one spring I attended an astronomy presentation by Jim Burr. The program featured a slide taken from the Hubbell Telescope, showing billions of stars millions of miles away. I gasped as I viewed the scene and heard the words as he read, "For as the heavens are higher than the earth, so are My ways higher than your ways, and My thoughts than your thoughts."

That slide presentation changed my life. I began to examine my activities during the day and do only the things the Lord directed me to, no more and no less. God is in control. He allows certain people to be elected to office at a given time, and his purposes are never hindered by their actions. We can sleep peacefully at night, knowing that God has everything completely under control.

Today's Prayer
Dear Heavenly Father, thank you for having a plan for our country and allowing us to be part of it. Thank you also for having a plan for our children. Help me to rest each night knowing I have done all that you have asked of me, no more and no less.

Just for Today
Gaze at the stars tonight and remind yourself that no matter how far away they are, God is in complete control.

SEVENTY-EIGHT

Y2K

Trust in the Lord with all your heart, and do not lean on your own understanding. In all your ways acknowledge Him, and He will make your paths straight.

PROVERBS 3:5-6

Depending upon when you are reading this, Y2K may have come and gone with little more than a yawn. In the later part of 1998 and at the beginning of 1999, however, it has been a major topic of conversation. Everyone has an opinion on the subject, with scenarios ranging from minor disruptions in public services to nuclear war.

When we first heard about the potential dangers Y2K could present to our family, we panicked. What should we do? Stockpile food? Buy guns? Seek shelter in some remote place? When we took our concerns to the Lord, however, we were reminded of some important principles of Scripture.

"For what does it profit a man to gain the whole world, and forfeit his soul?" (Mk 8:36). The Lord showed us that planning for the physical needs of our family was wise, but that planning for the spiritual needs of our family, friends, neighbors, and community was even more vital.

In school we researched all the potential disasters and came up with a plan to combat them. For instance, if the power were disrupted, what would we use as an alternative? We assessed our neighborhood. Most of our neighbors had a fireplace or woodstove, but some did not. How would we be able to help those people keep warm if there was no electricity?

The most exciting part about this study was seeing what we

could do for our neighbors. We began to realize that while Y2K had a great potential for disaster, it had an even greater potential for ministry and blessing. A wonderful opportunity may be on the horizon for Christians to practice their Christianity by giving food to the hungry, clothes to the naked, and a home to the homeless.

Today's Prayer

Dear Heavenly Father, Y2K has awakened us to potential needs around us. Show us how to meet those needs in a way that will bring honor and glory to you.

Just for Today

Talk to your children about going a whole day without electricity. Take one day and actually do so. Remind them of generations past who ate dinner and did school by candlelight.

SEVENTY-NINE

The Voice of God

And you said, Behold, the Lord our God has shown us His glory and His greatness, and we have heard His voice from the midst of the fire; we have seen today that God speaks with man, yet he lives.

DEUTERONOMY 5:24

I have always been fascinated with people in Scripture who heard the "voice of God" or the "voice of the Lord." As a new Christian, I asked a pastor if God would ever speak to me as he had to others in Scripture.

The pastor explained to me that God speaks only through his Word, and that hearing voices was not part of the Christian life today. I listened to what the pastor had to say, but something inside me hoped he was wrong. Many years later I learned that he was.

I was notorious for losing my keys, so much so that my husband attached a gadget to my key ring that would beep if you clapped or made a loud noise near it. One day while rushing to an appointment in Denver, I couldn't find my keys. I searched and clapped everywhere without success. After thirty stress-filled minutes I cried out loud to the Lord and said, "Oh, God, please help me find my keys!"

Just then a thought came into my mind: "Go outside, into the backyard, and look under the wagon." It wasn't an audible voice that I heard; it was a thought, an impression. It was so unusual that I followed the instructions and went into the backyard, clapping. A faint beep came from under the wagon. I thanked the Lord and rushed to my appointment.

Finding my keys was nothing compared to the discovery that God does speak to us and that we can hear his voice. Since then I have read the Bible and many other books that have helped me to understand how to hear God's voice and how to know when the enemy tries to counterfeit that voice.

Hearing the voice of God has become a part of our school program along with reading, writing, and arithmetic. Our children need to know not just how to talk to the Lord, but how to listen when he speaks. It is an area that needs much prayer and study but is well worth the time and effort.

Today's Prayer

Dear Heavenly Father, thank you for loving us enough to want to communicate with us in two-way conversation.

Just for Today

Turn on a fan and let your children speak into it. Listen to the changes in their voices.

EIGHTY

Day by Day

And he was saying to them all, "If anyone wishes to come after Me, let him deny himself, and take up his cross daily, and follow Me."
LUKE 9:23

After my daughter graduated from high school, a few years went by in which she seemed to float through life. She tried a few different jobs and took a couple of trips, but didn't seem happy or content.

In time we realized that we had spent eighteen years teaching her and preparing her to graduate from high school, but had not put much thought into what lay beyond. She was not led to college, she was not interested in a particular career, and a medical condition kept her from driving, so she stayed close to home.

About that same time we were desperate for someone to do data entry for our ministry but did not have a lot of extra money to hire someone full-time. We offered the job to her and began to train her in all that she needed to know. One day while praising her for a job well done we jokingly said, "If you keep this up, someday you'll become the office manager!"

Unknown to us at that time, those few words gave her a goal, and soon she began to take on more and more responsibility. Within a few short years she was able to order business cards with her name and, printed just below it, the words "Office Manager."

The problem we experienced with our daughter is common not only with high school seniors but with "senior saints" as well. Something seems to happen to the goals and dreams of many of these dear people once they hit sixty-five.

In some cases, these people seem to give up working in the church and building new relationships. "Ask someone else. I've done my time. Let one of the younger fellows take it on," they might say. With that, the church loses one of its most valuable resources—the maturity, experience, and wisdom of its older generation.

I have added a class in Post-Graduation/Retirement Studies to our school curriculum. It is important that our children understand that learning never stops, and neither does the work of the Lord.

When the Lord said, "Take up your cross daily and follow me," he did not mean only until you graduate or retire. Retirement opens doors for you to serve the Lord full-time. A well-rounded education includes instruction on opportunities to learn and serve that will last a lifetime.

Today's Prayer

Dear Heavenly Father, help our children catch a vision for all the things they can learn and do for you, whether they are three or one hundred and three.

Just for Today

Have your children call elderly saints in your church and interview them with regard to all the things they are learning and doing in their senior years.

EIGHTY-ONE

The Power of God

So he answered, "Do not fear, for those who are with us are more than those who are with them." Then Elisha prayed and said, "O Lord, I pray, open his eyes that he may see." And the Lord opened the servant's eyes, and he saw; and behold, the mountain was full of horses and chariots of fire all around Elisha.

2 KINGS 6:16-17

A good friend of mine told me that one year she and some others had tried to get legislation passed to make her state more "homeschool friendly." The measure died in committee.

The next fall she got a call from one of the state senators, who offered to help get a bill passed during the next session. He himself was not a homeschooler and was not a professing believer, but he was determined to help her with a new bill. He explained that his sleep had been troubled and that he felt compelled by some "force" to get involved. This man, along with his house counterpart, worked tirelessly to get the bill ready.

They met some resistance. Several homeschoolers found that their phones were being tapped, and one family had their home broken into (the only things taken were files related to the homeschool legislation). As their work continued, others received threatening phone calls and letters. In the end, however, the bill was passed, and families are now able to homeschool in that state without fear of imprisonment or fines.

As my friend looks back at the powerful forces that rose up against her and other homeschoolers, she can only say, as Elisha did in 2 Kings, "Do not fear, for those who are with us are more than those who are with them."

Hearing her story gives me added reason to believe that homeschooling is a movement ordained by God. He is the one who birthed it, has grown it, and protects it. We are humbled to be a part of it.

Today's Prayer

Dear Heavenly Father, it helps to hear about your mighty hand working on behalf of homeschooling families and that what you have ordained, you will maintain.

Just for Today

Pray and thank God for the homeschool pioneers who worked so hard to secure the laws we have that give us the freedom to homeschool today.

EIGHTY-TWO

Snow Day

He must increase, but I must decrease.　　　　　　　JOHN 3:30

The big week had come and our family was all excited. A major science conference had come to Denver and some of my children were enrolled in special classes where they would actually be able to touch dinosaur bones. Monday and Tuesday's conference sessions taught us all about creation and God's plan for the ages.

Wednesday was to be the final and best day. Not only were the children going to finally handle those dinosaur bones, but also our radio ministry was to be given a five-minute spotlight before four thousand people. When Wednesday morning arrived, however, with it came huge flakes of snow. Outside the skies looked ominous, but inside the cloud forming over my head was worse.

This couldn't be! This was our big day, and one by one the roads were closing. By noon the interstate was closed in both directions, and with it any hope of our attending the conference.

I stomped up to my room and muttered to myself as I took off my new dress, purchased just for this occasion. I was so wrapped up in self-pity that I almost missed the look on my children's faces. They, too, were crushed, but for a different reason. They were missing an opportunity to learn and explore, while I was missing an opportunity to ... to what? It hit me.

I was missing an opportunity to receive praise and glory that rightfully belonged only to the Lord! I wanted to go to hear the applause of men for something for which only the Lord truly deserved praise. Our broadcast and ministry have never been something we created or perfected. Yet here I was, all prepared to accept some awesome kudos for it. Father, forgive me!

How many times do we receive praise for God's work and rob him of what rightfully belongs to him? How often do we take credit for what our children accomplish and forget that he has made it all possible?

"Children," I said, "get your snowsuits on. We're going sledding. Come on ... I'll race you!" My boys couldn't believe their ears. Mom? Sledding?

The snowstorm had padded our sledding hill so that it was faster than ever. We sledded, made a snowman, built two snow forts, and pelted Dad with snowballs every time he poked his head out of the office door. What could have been the worst disappointment of the year turned out to be a day of reckoning and the best winter fun we've ever had!

Today's Prayer

Dear Father, thank you for the reminder that sometimes it takes a blizzard to help us see clearly.

Just for Today

Take time to build a winter snowman, gather some spring buds, play in a summer sandbox, or shuffle through the autumn leaves.

And there is salvation in no one else; for there is no other name under heaven that has been given among men, by which we must be saved.

ACTS 4:12

The Lord can use the strangest things to bring people to him. For my daughter, it was bathrooms. If we went into a restaurant or store when she was a little girl, the first thing she had to do was check out the bathroom. She would count the sinks, wash her hands, and make sure there was paper in every stall.

One evening at home she looked up at me and asked, "Mommy, will there be bathrooms in heaven?"

"Honey, if you need a bathroom in heaven, I'm sure it will be there."

She pondered my answer for a minute or two, then asked, "Mommy, will there be bathrooms in hell?"

Mentally scanning all the sermons I had ever heard on the subject of hell, I said, "Honey, I am sure that if you need a bathroom in hell it won't be there. There will be nothing in hell to give you any relief or comfort."

"Mommy, can you please tell me how I can become a Christian and go to heaven? I don't ever want to go to hell!"

For the next few minutes her father and I shared with her how Jesus, the Son of God, came to earth as a baby, grew up, and paid the price for our sin by dying on the cross. We invited her to pray and thank God for dying for her and paying the price for her sin personally. She did, and at that moment she received God's gift of forgiveness, and secured her place in heaven for all eternity.

There is no greater privilege than to be able to lead one of your children to the Lord Jesus Christ. After she prayed, we talked about what she'd like to do once she got to heaven and saw God. Innocently she looked at me and said, "Check out the bathrooms!"

Today's Prayer

Dear Heavenly Father, thank you for sending your Son to die on the cross so we would have the ability to receive him and spend eternity with you in heaven.

Just for Today

Do you know for sure that if you were to die today you would spend eternity with God in heaven? What about your children? If you or they have never given your lives to Jesus Christ, do it today.

EIGHTY-FOUR

Hall of Fame

Therefore, since we have so great a cloud of witnesses surrounding us, let us also lay aside every encumbrance, and the sin which so easily entangles us, and let us run with endurance the race that is set before us.

HEBREWS 12:1

I began a dreary, winter school day with the following question: "What do Thomas Jefferson, James Madison, Patrick Henry, Florence Nightingale, Robert E. Lee, Thomas Edison, Irving Berlin, and C.S. Lewis all have in common?"

The children thought for a few minutes, tried to classify each of the names with which they were familiar, and racked their brains to find the common thread. Finally one of the children shouted, "I've got it! They're all dead!"

Although he was correct, that was not the answer I was looking for. "They were all homeschooled!" I finally revealed. Moans and groans met me. As I began to give brief biographies of these people, along with a few others, the children's attention increased. These presidents, authors, scientists, and nurses all got their start at home. This thought connected my children to these heroes of the past. It inspired them to keep doing what they were doing and gave them role models to look up to.

After reading that list to them, I read another list: Abraham, Isaac, Jacob, Joseph, Moses, Rahab, Gideon, Barak, Samson, Jephthah, David, Samuel, and the prophets. According to Hebrews 11 these were people who by faith conquered kingdoms, performed acts of righteousness, shut the mouths of lions, quenched the power of fire, escaped the edge of the sword, and put foreign armies to flight. As I read their brief biographies, the children could see some even greater role models.

Sometimes it is hard to hang in there when you feel like you are the only one, whether it's homeschooling in your neighborhood or being a Christian in your community. When our faith is low, we need assurances that there are others who have gone before us, attempted the same thing, and succeeded.

Are there people in our circles who need to see our successes in order to find the courage they need to continue what God has called them to do? Could we someday be the necessary spiritual "link" to lead another to Christ, keep a family together, or put a foreign army to flight?

Maybe the day wasn't so dreary, after all.

Today's Prayer

O Father in heaven, thank you for the names and faces of faithful saints before us. Help us live today in a way that will be encouraging to someone one hundred years from now.

Just for Today

Go around the room and have each person tell about someone living today who influenced him or her in a positive way. Write a thank-you letter to that person.

EIGHTY-FIVE

It's Nice to Know You

More than that, I count all things to be loss in the view of the surpassing value of knowing Christ Jesus my Lord, for whom I have suffered the loss of all things, and count them but rubbish in order that I may gain Christ.

PHILIPPIANS 3:8

One day as we were working on a science project in the schoolroom, Dad poked his head in the door and said, "I just got a message from Mr. Johnson. He wants all of you children to meet with him today." With that, Dad exited the room.

"Who's Mr. Johnson?" Connie asked.

"Yeah," the rest echoed, "who is he?"

I didn't know who Mr. Johnson was, either, but it was certain that we couldn't continue with science as long as this puzzle existed. We left the schoolroom and found Dad sitting in the living room with a Bible.

"Dad, who is Mr. Johnson, and why does he want to see us?"

Dad asked us all to sit down. "The fact is, children, you do not know Mr. Johnson. If you knew him, you would know exactly where to go and what time to be there.

"For instance, suppose you were in the Civil Air Patrol and had regular meetings with your commanding officer every Tuesday evening in Denver. Now, if Major Forrest's secretary left a message that you were to bring a certain report to your 6:30 meeting, you would immediately know that she was referring to your meeting in Denver. That is where you meet Major Forrest every Tuesday."

Although I wasn't sure what point Terry was trying to make, I was sure Major Forrest wasn't really the issue. My husband went on. "This morning I watched you as Mom taught you your Bible lesson. Some of you doodled on paper, one played with a truck, and one poked holes in a piece of cardboard lying nearby. I didn't see you paying close attention, as you need to. Reading the Bible and spending time with the Lord is something we do every day, not just once a week, because that is what it takes to get to know him—and to understand what he wants us to do."

Dad's object lesson sank in, and from that day on there seemed to be a new enthusiasm in all of us when it came to our Bible classes and devotions. We are all getting to know him much better.

Today's Prayer

Heavenly Father, we're so glad we met you. Help us to continue really getting to know you.

Just for Today

Have the children practice greeting someone new with a smile and a firm handshake.

EIGHTY-SIX

The Image of God

Then God said, "Let Us make man in Our image, according to Our likeness." GENESIS 1:26a

We were going through Genesis in detail when we came to the phrase "Let Us make man in Our image."

"Just what is the image of God?" seven-year-old Helen inquired. I was stuck! We got out five commentaries and got five different answers.

At that moment ten-year-old James spoke up. "Why not take everyone's face who is living in the world, load their image into the computer, superimposed one over another, and come up with one picture? Maybe that picture would be the image of God!"

For the rest of the day we pondered the question and tried to understand what the phrase "image of God" meant. I realized that this was one of those times when I had to tell my children that we would not be able to fully understand this concept until we were in heaven. Still, I wished that I had a more satisfying answer for them.

Just after lunch, two of the children got into a verbal battle over a toy. When one of them had had enough, he hauled off and hit his brother. Immediately the wounded child responded with, "You just struck the image of God!" You could have heard a pin drop in the kitchen. As soon as the full impact of what was said sunk in, the offender, speaking in a soft voice, said, "I'm sorry," and handed over the toy.

That morning in school we had tried very hard to research and understand "the image of God" with our heads but never could. When it came down to true understanding, the lesson had to be learned in our hearts.

Today's Prayer

O Heavenly Father, we are made in the "image of God." What an awesome concept to understand! Help us to look at each other always with that phrase in mind.

Just for Today

Make a silhouette picture by hanging up a sheet of paper and shining a lamp onto it. Take turns sitting in front of the lamp and letting each other trace the silhouettes onto a piece of paper.

EIGHTY-SEVEN
The Mercy of God

The Lord is good to all, and His mercies are over all His works.
PSALM 145:9

While going through one of my children's math books, I realized that he had not been completing all of his work for some time. I had been giving him his assignment and had planned to correct his work every day or so, but I had gotten behind. Over three weeks had gone by since I had last checked on his progress, and I was more than disappointed to learn that he had skipped sections and hastily written answers in others.

I went through each page with him, making notes as to what he needed to complete, and noticed a heaviness begin to droop his shoulders. He was feeling overwhelmed by the amount of time it would take to correct nearly a month's worth of material. When I finished, he sat down, defeated before he even began.

I was troubled as I watched him, so I began to pray. "Father, what's wrong with this picture?"

"Mercy!" was the only response.

I began to argue. "But, Lord, he deceived me. My son led me to believe he had been completing his work all this time while he hadn't. For me to show him mercy would be letting him get away with sin!"

"Mercy!"

"Now, Lord, he knew what he was supposed to do, but he didn't do it. What message will I be sending him if I wipe out all his consequences?"

"The same message I sent you!"

Suddenly my anger and frustration abated, and I called my son to my side. I told him about a time in my life when, even though I was a Christian, I disobeyed God, got myself into a real pickle, and was overwhelmed with guilt and a sense of hopelessness. A friend talked to me and reminded me that the Lord's mercies were new every morning. Although I couldn't erase the mistakes of the past, I could get a fresh beginning that day. So I asked the Lord's forgiveness for my past failure and pressed on.

"Why don't we do the same?" I asked him. With tears in his eyes he gave me a big hug and prayed, asking God to forgive him for his laziness and deception.

It's amazing how that simple act of mercy had the opposite effect from what I had feared. Grateful for the mercy shown him, he worked harder than ever from that point on and never repeated his deed.

Today's Prayer

O Lord, thank you for the mercy you show us every day when we fail to meet your standards. Thank you for opportunities to demonstrate that mercy in the lives of others.

Just for Today

Buy a bucket of ice cream and some cones and serve up treats to the children. Then sit and talk about all the times you have received pardon, grace, and mercy.

EIGHTY-EIGHT
Name That Country!

Woe to those who enact evil statutes, and to those who constantly record unjust decisions, so as to deprive the needy of justice, and rob the poor of My people of their rights, in order that widows may be their spoil, and that they may plunder the orphans.

ISAIAH 10:1-2

Trying to teach children about the complicated systems of government can be quite a challenge. I pored through resources trying to find something that would put together the whole picture of how a country is run, but could find nothing.

One day the Lord gave me an idea. "Children," I announced, "today you have been given a very special gift. You have been given the opportunity to create your own country. Use this gift wisely and it will bless you. Use the gift foolishly and many lives could be hurt."

Naming the country, designing its borders, and creating its wealth was a blast, but as they got into the operations of the country, things began to get more serious. What form of government should it have? Should it be a democracy? A representative republic? A dictatorship? What laws should be passed in this country? And on what basis should the laws be made?

Creating their own country was just the ticket to learning about systems of government, but it created a dilemma. The more they researched what they believed a government should look like based on biblical principles, the more they realized how far short our nation has fallen from that ideal.

We began to read the paper with new vision, looking for encouraging signs but finding few. Law after law being passed seemed to afflict the needy and the powerless rather than encourage what was good or right. This exercise began to work in the hearts of the children and prompt them to pray for their leaders and dream of becoming a senator or even president someday.

It is not enough to learn the facts, figures, and statistics about a subject; those facts need to move us to action. Looking at government through a biblical worldview can spur us on to correct what is wrong in our nation. Seeing the faults in our system can leave our children with feelings of antagonism and futility—or excitement about what they can do to change things for the better.

Today's Prayer

Dear Lord, how we pray for our nation and our leaders. Remind them daily of what is right, and help them make good choices for our nation.

Just for Today

Have the children choose one government leader, politician, or judge for whom to pray. Have them write a letter to that person communicating their support, and watch the news and papers daily to see how God is working in that person's life.

EIGHTY-NINE

You Can't Please Everyone

Jesus said, "Truly I say to you, there is no one who has left house or brothers or sisters or mother or father or children or farms, for My sake and for the gospel's sake, but that he shall receive a hundred times as much now in the present age, houses and brothers and sisters and mothers and children and farms, along with persecutions; and in the age to come, eternal life."

MARK 10:29-30

The phone at the office rang one day, and at the other end was the voice of a desperate man. Apparently his parents had bitterly opposed his decision to homeschool for the past two years, and during the summer they had threatened to call social services if this man chose to homeschool again.

Now it was November and his folks were planning to come to his home for Thanksgiving. The man was in a panic. He had no doubt that his own mother would indeed call social services.

Terry learned that this man had spent a great deal of time and effort, trying to educate his parents about his homeschooling choice, but the grandparents would not budge. The advice Terry gave this man came as somewhat of a shock, but he took it.

He called his mother and told her point-blank that he was homeschooling his children. He reminded her that he loved his children very much and was doing what he thought was best for them. He finished the conversation by telling his parents that if they could not be supportive of his homeschooling decision, they would not be welcome in his home for the holidays.

"Well, we didn't realize you felt this strongly about it!" the mother replied. Grandma and Grandpa came for the holidays, and after seeing the results of homeschooling firsthand, they returned home and began a crusade in the family to have all their grandchildren homeschooled.

Not all family conflicts have such good results. Some grandparents are still not speaking to their children over their homeschooling decision, which has resulted in deep wounds. This is particularly bad in families where the grandparents were educators themselves and see no problem with the current public school system, which was "good enough for them." We must do what we can to keep the lines of communication open with family and friends. Yet, remember that the call to homeschool may come at a very high price.

Today's Prayer

Dear Lord, thank you for well-meaning friends and family who have sometimes challenged our homeschooling decisions. Give us the courage to face them and stand strong.

Just for Today

Have the children write a letter to their grandparents or to a family member who may need a bit of encouragement.

NINETY

The Greatest Compliment

Keep your behavior excellent among the Gentiles, so that in the thing in which they slander you as evildoers, they may on account of your good deeds, as they observe them, glorify God in the day of visitation.

1 Peter 2:12

While approaching the schoolroom door one morning I heard little voices coming from the lighted room. "What a lovely 'E,'" five-year-old Connie cooed to four-year-old Anna. "You made this letter even better than I could!" she encouraged.

"Now let's move on to the letter 'N,'" she continued. "I'm sure you won't have trouble with this. But if you do, I will help you."

They were obviously playing school, so I stayed by the door to hear what else they'd do. Connie helped Anna with letters and subjects that she barely had a handle on herself, and what she didn't know she just made up.

I choked back giggles when Connie told Anna she needed to take a coffee break with a "double mocha decaf, extra dry." I was reduced to gelatin when Anna announced that when she grew up she wanted to be a mommy with lots of kids, and that she was going to homeschool them all!

As Connie pretended to be "me," I was amazed at how kind and patient she was as the "teacher." Was this really how she saw me? What about all the times I was short-tempered? Or the times I had to be asked twice to help because I was too busy working on some letter or office work?

Listening to my girls play school brought tears to my eyes as I thought about how my heavenly Father did the same. Neither he nor they were keeping a record of my shortcomings and failures. All they saw was the good.

It's been said, "Imitation is the sincerest form of flattery." That day I received one of the greatest compliments my children could give me. Despite all my flaws, mistakes, and inadequacies, they wanted to be just like me!

Today's Prayer

O Father in heaven, help us live our lives so that Christ will be seen in us and our children will be drawn to him.

Just for Today

Play Simon Says with your children. If you begin a command with "Simon Says," they must do it, but if you issue a command without it, they have to ignore your command or be "out."

Scripture Verses